THE OFFICIAL

COOKBOOK

THE OFFICIAL

COOKBOOK

BY TOM GRIMM & JESSIE HASSETT

PHOTOGRAPHY BY
TOM GRIMM & DIMITRIE HARDER

London

An Insight Editions Book

Contents

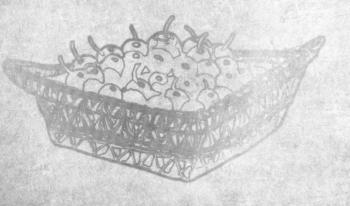

Sides

Sweet Delights

Baked Goods

Drinks & Potions

Dear Mum,

It's me, Devon! I'm all grown up now—or, well, more grown up than before. You always said I was too much like a child for my own good, and given the number of times you caught me daydreaming about going off on some grand adventure instead of sweeping the floors, I will grudgingly admit that you probably—probably—had a point. But guess what? I finally went on an adventure! A big one! Just like the Hero of Ferelden!

Okay, well, maybe not exactly like the Hero of Ferelden. But I did travel across Thedas! From Ferelden to Orlais, to Rivain, to even Tevinter. Plus, everything in between. It was a long journey, Mum. Weeks and weeks on the road, with the occasional bandit or beast. You'd probably have hated it, but, by Andraste, I loved every second of it! The sights! The sounds! The food.

Oh yes, the food. The reason why I set out on this journey to begin with. I know that I wasn't particularly adept in the kitchen the last time we saw each other. And, yes, I do remember that I nearly set Castle Cousland aflame with my first attempt at a stew. But I am pleased to inform you that I have been practicing extensively, and I think that, if the position still existed, I could take up your mantle as the Cousland family's cook. Granted, I doubt I would be able to fill your shoes completely; no one could manage such an impossible task. But I like to tell myself that I still would be able to make you proud.

And that takes me back to this journey and the all-important question of why. Why did I spend the last year traveling from one end of Thedas to the other, sampling whatever local cuisine I could get my hands on, even dishes that were downright strange? You're probably thinking that it's because the Hero of Ferelden ate it at some point—yes, that's certainly part of it, though I'll have you know that I tracked down foods enjoyed by the Champion of Kirkwall and the Inquisitor as well! Not to mention all of their companions. But the truth is, Mum, throughout all of this, you were right there with them at the forefront of my mind. Because when I thought of ways to honor you, I kept coming back to the most important lesson you taught me: Love through food.

Every time I left your kitchen with a warm, full belly, I felt your love for me. And though I can't do the same for you anymore, I can fill this book. I can stuff it full of different recipes, dishes you've probably never even heard of, and think of you with each new entry. Because, you see, Mum, underneath all that childlike excitement, the dreams of adventure and heroism, I'm still very much your child. And I always will be.

Thank you for everything, Mum. I can't wait to share this book and the lesson that inspired it with the rest of the world.

Love,
Devon

Starters & Refreshments

Eggs à la Val Foret

Ah, yes. Tons of cream! Exactly what I've come to expect from Orlesian cuisine. Do I have any tips for creating the perfect poached egg? Well, ever since I heard that Solas's bald head was once likened to an egg, I simply try to make my eggs just as round and shiny! So far, it's worked wonderfully and never ceases to put a smile on my face.

Yield	Cook time	Difficulty
2 SERVINGS	15 MINUTES	AVERAGE

Ingredients

5 tablespoons vinegar

2 eggs, as fresh as possible

1 English muffin

2 tablespoons hollandaise sauce (store-bought)

Sliced ham or Canadian bacon, to taste

Salt

Paprika

Fresh parsley, minced

1 Heat 8 cups of water in a medium pot over high heat. Add the vinegar. When the water boils, lower the heat to low and allow it to cool a bit. The water should be hot but no longer boiling.

2 Use a whisk to create a whirlpool in the water. Then crack the eggs and drop them into the whirlpool, one at a time. Make sure the water is moving when the eggs drop in. Cover the pot, and cook the eggs for 3 to 5 minutes, depending on how runny or firm you like your yolk.

3 Use a slotted spoon or skimmer to carefully remove the eggs from the pot. Set them on paper towels to drain.

4 Cut the English muffin in half and toast both halves.

5 Heat the hollandaise in the microwave.

6 Set each half of the English muffin on a plate, cut side up. Top with sliced ham, then set one poached egg on each. Sprinkle with salt, paprika, and a bit of freshly chopped parsley.

If you have trouble poaching the eggs, don't drop them "naked" into the pot. Instead, form a little package for each one out of plastic wrap. Close the package securely so no water can get inside, and then cook the eggs as described here but for 1 minute longer than noted, depending on your desired consistency. In this case, there is no need to add the vinegar or to swirl the water.

Nevarran Blood Orange Salad

Although I knew that Divine Victoria left behind a life of wealth and privilege to join the Seekers of Truth, it wasn't until I was in Nevarra, seeing exactly what she'd given up, that I truly gained an appreciation for the path she'd chosen. The best way to describe my first glimpse of the gardens of Nevarra is that it was like seeing a painting come to life. For a long moment, I could only stand there, so dazzled by the richness and vibrancy of it all that I was half-convinced I was actually still napping in the carriage. Surely, there was no way such beauty could be found outside of a dream. And yet the beauty before me was very much real.

So, too, was the picturesque tableau that arrived later that day on a plate: perfectly cut slices of blood orange artfully arranged on a lush pillow of bitter greens. Was this a meal or a still life, I wondered. In truth, the answer was both. For Nevarrans, food is as much a feast for the eyes as for the mouth. But even if your arrangement isn't quite worthy of being displayed in a museum, this salad will sing a symphony on your tastebuds!

Yield	Cook time	Difficulty
4 SERVINGS	15 MINUTES	AVERAGE

Ingredients

4 blood oranges

3 tablespoons raspberry vinegar

2 tablespoons agave syrup

2 tablespoons walnut oil

1 teaspoon salt

1 teaspoon pepper

6 cups mixed salad (such as lamb's lettuce or spring mix)

3 cups radicchio, thinly sliced

1 spring onion (or scallion/green onion), cut into thin rings

½ cup pine nuts

1 Peel the oranges, then use a small sharp knife to cut out the rounds. Catch the juice in the process.

2 Combine the orange juice, raspberry vinegar, agave syrup, and walnut oil in a small bowl. Season with the salt and pepper.

3 Transfer the mixed salad, radicchio, and spring onions (or scallion/green onion) to a bowl. Pour the dressing over the salad and carefully toss.

4 Divide the salad among four serving bowls, garnish each one with a few orange segments, and serve sprinkled with pine nuts.

Fried Young Giant Spiders

Just as people on the surface raise cows and goats, the dwarves underground raise spiders. Yes, to eat. The legs are fried and served with sauce, which, in true dwarven fashion, is made with some type of alcohol. The precise kind depends on the establishment where you're eating your spider legs. Unfortunately, I couldn't get an exact recipe from any of the chefs I spoke to. These sauces are apparently closely guarded secrets and have spurred many a nefarious plot to acquire them—the competition to be crowned Orzammar's Best Sauce is fierce. But I've been assured that lichen ale is generally not used.

I've therefore come up with my own recipe, based on the many varieties I sampled while in Orzammar. Given that sourcing the requisite spider legs above ground is not nearly so easy, and the demand for such exports is minimal, I've substituted them with crab legs. It's not a perfect match, but it's close enough to satisfy me.

Yield	Cook time	Difficulty
4 SERVINGS	25 MINUTES	AVERAGE

Ingredients

4 king crab legs
(each about 10.5 ounces)

4 tablespoons olive oil

4 garlic cloves, minced

2 shallots, minced

1 red chili pepper,
sliced into thin rings

Salt

Juice of 1 lemon

1   Preheat the oven to 390°F. Line two baking sheets with parchment paper.

2   Wash the crab legs, and use kitchen shears to separate them at the joints. Cut open the crab pieces lengthwise on one side.

3   Heat 1 tablespoon olive oil in a large, oven-safe frying pan over medium heat. Add the sets of crab legs one at a time and carefully brown on all sides (about 2 to 3 minutes). Add one-quarter of the garlic, shallot, and chili pepper to each set of crab legs; then cook all ingredients together briefly (about 2 minutes), and season the crab with salt to taste. Set two crab legs on each prepared baking sheet, together with the onions, garlic, and chili.

4   Cook the crab legs in the preheated oven for 5 minutes. Then remove, drizzle each with one-quarter of the lemon juice, and serve immediately. Wait until the dish is at the table to remove the crab meat from the shell.

Stuffed Deep Mushrooms

Though the mushrooms growing underground in caves and in many parts of the Deep Roads are all called "deep mushrooms," there is no singular variety. In fact, there are several! Some mushrooms are squat, with broad, flat caps, while others are long and spindly, reaching up toward the sky like an old man's gnarled fingers. They also have a multitude of applications, used in the creation of everything from restorative potions to deadly poisons. But in Orzammar, mushrooms are farmed for eating!

I was able to sample some of these dwarven delicacies, prized for their unique flavor and intoxicating scent. After only a few bites, I was struck with inspiration. How delicious would one of these mushrooms be when stuffed with cheese and spinach? The answer is: very. Rest assured that I selected this particular variety of deep mushroom not only for its shape, which is ideal for holding the maximum amount of cheese (and spinach), but also for the fact that it does not carry the darkspawn taint. While certain dwarves will insist that a deep mushroom's proximity to lyrium and darkspawn can only improve its flavor, I am quite content to leave that particular question a mystery, especially where lyrium is concerned. Although I'm hardly an expert on the stuff, I can't help but think about Fenris and how much suffering he endured as a result of his lyrium-infused markings. It seems to me that, barring any natural resistance, lyrium and the body are two things that probably shouldn't mix.

Yield	Cook time	Difficulty
4 SERVINGS	20 MINUTES	AVERAGE

Ingredients

4 large portobello mushrooms

7 ounces herb cream cheese or Boursin cheese

½ shallot, minced

1 cup baby spinach, finely chopped

Salt

Pepper

⅓ cup shredded cheese (such as Cheddar or Gouda)

Fresh chives, minced

1 Preheat the oven to 300°F. Line a baking sheet with parchment paper.

2 Carefully clean the mushrooms, and remove the stems with a small, sharp knife. Then carefully hollow out the mushrooms a bit.

3 Combine the cream cheese with the shallot and baby spinach in a small bowl, and season generously with salt and pepper.

4 Fill the mushrooms with the cream cheese mixture, smooth the tops, and sprinkle with a bit of shredded cheese. Set the mushrooms on the prepared baking sheet, and bake for about 12 to 15 minutes or until the mushrooms are done and the cheese is melted. If the cheese darkens too much before the mushrooms are cooked, cover loosely with aluminum foil and continue baking.

5 Set the cooked mushrooms on a plate lined with paper towels to drain briefly. To serve, sprinkle with a bit of minced chives. Enjoy promptly.

Rivaini Couscous Salad

When I first encountered couscous, I mistakenly believed it to be a grain, like rice or the more familiar Fereldan barley. I was swiftly corrected. In fact, couscous is a sort of pasta, made with semolina flour and water, although it's far smaller than your typical Antivan pasta. Couscous has a very mild flavor on its own—maybe slightly nutty. But where it excels is in its ability to soak up surrounding flavors, making it a perfect base for any salad. I'd love to experiment further, but so far, this particular combination of red bell pepper and mint has proven to be incredibly pleasing.

Yield	Cook time	Difficulty
4 SERVINGS	40 MINUTES	AVERAGE

Ingredients

½ cup plus 1 tablespoon vegetable broth

½ cup couscous

1 tablespoon honey

2 tablespoons plus 2 teaspoons lemon juice

Generous pinch ground cumin

4 tablespoons olive oil

1 tablespoon parsley, minced

Salt

Pepper

1 garlic clove, minced

1 spring onion (or scallion/green onion), cut into thin rings

½ red bell pepper, diced

½ green bell pepper, diced

7 ounces chickpeas (canned), drained

Squeeze of lemon juice

Fresh mint, for garnishing

1   Transfer the broth to a small pot, and heat over medium heat.

2   Place the couscous in a bowl large enough to hold it and pour the warm broth over it. Stir well to combine, and allow to stand for 10 to 15 minutes or until the couscous has absorbed all the liquid. Fluff with a fork.

3   Transfer the honey, lemon juice, cumin, 4 tablespoons olive oil, and parsley to a bowl large enough to hold the ingredients, and stir well to combine. Season generously with salt and pepper.

4   Add the garlic, spring onions (or scallion/green onion), red and green bell peppers, and chickpeas to the bowl containing the vinaigrette, and stir well to combine. Allow to stand for 15 minutes. Then mix the couscous into the remaining ingredients, and drizzle with a squeeze of lemon juice.

5   Serve garnished with a bit of fresh mint.

Crab Cakes from Kirkwall

I love it when recipes add a dash of whimsy into the mix. Food should be fun. I, therefore, took it upon myself to put this into practice with a classic Kirkwall dish. After all, who hasn't looked at their crab cakes and wished they looked a little more like crabs? Okay, maybe I'm the only one who's thought this. But now that I've brought this possibility to your attention, I'm certain you're interested as well! Best of all, these extra-crabby crab cakes stay true to the original recipe's flavors, so nothing is lost—only gained!

Yield	Cook time	Difficulty
4 SERVINGS	ABOUT 30 TO 45 MINUTES (DEPENDING ON PAN SIZE)	AVERAGE

Ingredients

¾ cup plus 4 teaspoons flour

2¼ cups bread crumbs

¾ cup plus 2 tablespoons cornstarch

1 tablespoon salt

1 tablespoon pepper

3 eggs

2 pounds soft-shell crab

Oil, for frying

1 onion, diced

4 garlic cloves, minced

1 piece fresh ginger root (a little less than 1¼ inches), minced

1 red chili, sliced into thin rings

3.5 ounces Thai chili paste

Juice of 1 lemon

Equipment
Kitchen thermometer

1 Mix the flour, bread crumbs, cornstarch, salt, and pepper in a shallow bowl.

2 Crack the eggs into a separate shallow bowl, and beat.

3 Dredge the crabs in the flour mixture until they're coated on all sides. Dredge the crabs in the egg, and dredge again in the flour mixture. Set the breaded crab on a large plate.

4 Heat an inch of oil in as large a frying pan as possible over high heat until the oil reaches 350°F. When the oil has reached the proper temperature, add the crabs in batches with a metal slotted spoon or skimmer and deep-fry until golden (about 3 to 4 minutes), turning once halfway through. Set the crabs on a plate lined with paper towels to drain. Add fresh oil to the pan as needed until all the crabs are fried.

5 Drain, rinse, and wipe out the pan, and heat 1 tablespoon of oil in it over medium heat. Add the onion, garlic, ginger, and chili and sweat (about 2 minutes). Stir in the chili paste, and sauté all the ingredients together for 1 minute. Add the fried crabs in batches, carefully swirl, and heat again briefly (2 to 3 minutes).

6 Drizzle with lemon juice and enjoy promptly.

> The shell and claws of soft-shell crabs are soft enough that they can be eaten with no problem.

Fluffy Mackerel Pudding

Can it really be Feast Day without fluffy mackerel pudding? No! In fact, there's no dish I associate more strongly with the holiday than this unique combination of mackerel, onion, celery, and eggs. Granted, I've heard stories that, several decades ago, someone once attempted a diet consisting entirely of fluffy mackerel pudding. Now, that I certainly wouldn't recommend. It stops being Feast Day Fish if you eat it every day, no?

Yield	Cook time	Difficulty
4 SERVINGS	1 HOUR (INCLUDING BAKING)	AVERAGE

Ingredients

1 pound potatoes
(russet or similar),
peeled and coarsely diced

Salt

8.8 ounces smoked mackerel
fillets, coarsely chopped

3½ tablespoons butter, softened

2 eggs

Freshly ground black pepper

1 hard-boiled egg, thinly sliced

Grated nutmeg

Equipment

Potato masher

4 small soufflé molds

1 Generously salt a large pot of water and place it over medium heat. Bring to a boil. Add the potatoes and cook for 20 minutes or until the potatoes are cooked and tender. Drain the potatoes in a strainer, leaving them briefly to drip thoroughly.

2 Transfer the potatoes to a medium bowl and coarsely mash with a potato masher. Add the mackerel fillets, butter, and eggs, and combine with an electric mixer or stand mixer until the ingredients form a fluffy mass. Season generously with salt and pepper.

3 Preheat the oven to 350°F. Set the soufflé molds on a baking sheet.

4 Fill the molds with the potato-and-fish mixture, then smooth the tops and bake on the middle rack for about 30 to 35 minutes until golden. Remove from the oven and garnish each pudding with one egg slice. Sprinkle with a bit of grated nutmeg to taste.

5 Enjoy while still warm.

Snail & Watercress Salad

When the Avvar can't get their hands on a gurgut or wyvern, they turn their attention to smaller prey. Much smaller prey. Snails are found on many a hillside boulder, making them an abundant source of food for the Avvar. Now, while some would wrinkle their noses or cry out in disgust at the prospect of eating a snail, I am pleased to report that, when prepared correctly, the texture and flavor are actually good! I could happily eat a plate full of snails dressed in butter and oil, but those still on the fence about a snail's place in Lowlander cuisine might prefer to sample them in conjunction with other ingredients. Might I suggest a snail and watercress salad? It's not exactly traditional Avvar cuisine, but my hosts certainly seemed to enjoy it!

Yield	Cook time	Difficulty
4 SERVINGS	25 MINUTES	AVERAGE

Ingredients

1 red onion, diced

10 cups mixed salad
(such as lamb's lettuce,
spring mix, and arugula)

1 bunch radishes, thinly sliced

3 tablespoons canola oil

1 to 2 teaspoons Dijon mustard
(or other medium-spicy
mustard)

Pinch of sugar

3 tablespoons herb vinegar

Salt

Pepper

4.5 ounces canned escargots,
drained

2 tablespoons butter

2 garlic cloves, minced

1 Combine the onion, salad, and radishes in a medium bowl.

2 Stir the oil, mustard, sugar, and vinegar together in a small bowl. Season to taste with pepper and salt.

3 Pour the dressing over the salad. Toss so the salad is coated with dressing and allow to stand for 15 minutes for the flavors to meld.

4 Meanwhile, put the escargots in a strainer and rinse thoroughly in cold running water. Drain and carefully pat dry with paper towels.

5 Melt the butter in a frying pan over medium heat. Add the garlic and sweat briefly (1 minute). Add the escargots and brown on all sides for 3 to 4 minutes. Season to taste with salt and pepper.

6 Divide the salad among four serving bowls, divide the escargots between them, and serve immediately.

7 This dish is excellent with a baguette or similar bread on the side.

Cave Beetles

You think that, after snails, I'd balk at beetles? Never! In fact, I greatly enjoyed this dwarven dish, which involves roasting cave beetles in their shells. However, I recognize that many may not have a palate that's nearly so adventurous. If that's the case, the cave beetles can be replaced with whole prawns while keeping the rest of the recipe the same. That being said, if you do enjoy the variation with prawns, I really recommend giving the cave beetles a try. They're quite similar in both texture and flavor. If you were to blindfold yourself, I doubt you could tell the difference!

Yield	Cook time	Difficulty
4 SERVINGS	20 MINUTES	AVERAGE

Ingredients

12 prawns
4 garlic cloves, finely pressed
4 tablespoons olive oil
4 tablespoons white wine
2 tablespoons lemon juice
1 teaspoon salt
1 teaspoon chili powder
Lemon wedges, for serving

Equipment
Casserole dish
(about 9½ by 12½ inches)

1 Preheat the oven to 425°F.

2 Briefly rinse the prawns in cold water, and pat dry with paper towels. Arrange the prawns side by side in a casserole dish large enough to hold them.

3 Combine the garlic, olive oil, white wine, lemon juice, salt, and chili powder in a small bowl. Pour evenly over the prawns in the casserole dish.

4 Bake in the preheated oven for about 7 to 8 minutes (for raw prawns) or 3 to 4 minutes (for precooked prawns). Remove from the dish, arrange them on a large plate, and serve with lemon wedges. Enjoy promptly.

For the Road

Spiced Jerky

Preserved foods play an important role in many different cultures across Thedas. Not only do they help certain communities weather times of scarcity brought on by the changing of the seasons, but they also ensure that long journeys away from home are possible. Imagine how difficult it would be for Dalish hunters to bring back meat the clan is depending on if they have to be back for supper every night—or, worse, hunt on an empty stomach! This spiced jerky ensures that all Dalish hunters are well provisioned whenever they set out on a hunt so that no one, either the hunter or the clan at home, must go hungry.

I do wonder, given how well this food keeps, whether it's used in offerings made by certain Dalish elves to Fen'Harel. Although his shrines are usually located well outside of Dalish camps, I can't imagine that leaving behind food that'll readily spoil is good practice, especially if the prevailing opinion about these shrines is to avoid them. Besides, he is the Dread Wolf. If any god would enjoy a good piece of jerky, it should be him!

Yield	Cook time	Difficulty
ABOUT 12 OUNCES OF JERKY	20+ HOURS (INCLUDING MARINATING AND DRYING)	AVERAGE

Ingredients

2 pounds lean beef, such as round or flank steak (no more than ¼ inch thick)

8 tablespoons soy sauce

2 tablespoons teriyaki sauce

2 tablespoons Worcestershire sauce

1 tablespoon Tabasco

1 teaspoon garlic powder

2 tablespoons Sichuan peppercorns, finely crushed

1 tablespoon chili flakes

1 Rinse the steaks, and pat dry with paper towels. Working on a cutting board, cut across the grain into rectangular pieces of your desired size (about 6 inches wide).

2 In a small bowl, combine the soy sauce, teriyaki sauce, Worcestershire sauce, Tabasco, garlic powder, and Sichuan pepper.

3 Transfer the marinade and meat to a freezer bag. Massage the marinade into the meat, and marinate for at least 12 hours in the refrigerator (or longer, if desired).

4 Remove the meat from the marinade, and carefully pat dry with paper towels. Arrange the meat on an oven rack so that the pieces do not touch, and place in the oven at 100°F. (Preheating is not necessary.) If your oven does not have such low temperature settings, set it to the lowest possible temperature. While drying, insert the handle of a wooden spoon into the oven door so that it stays open a crack and the moisture generated inside can escape.

5 Dry the meat in the oven for 4 hours, then turn and dry for another 3 to 4 hours or until the jerky is as firm to the bite as desired. Remove from the oven, allow to cool completely, and sprinkle generously with chili flakes.

6 Transfer to an airtight sealed container. Preferably, allow it to rest for 1 or 2 more days before consuming so that the remaining moisture can spread evenly through the meat. Spiced jerky will keep this way for several weeks.

Grey Warden Pastry Pockets

Unlike many of us, Grey Wardens often don't have the luxury of sitting down for their meals. Instead, they're off on patrol, usually in less-than-pleasant climates, which makes their work all the more exhausting. In their shoes, I imagine I'd be downright ravenous, well beyond what a handful of nuts could hope to sate. But a pastry stuffed to the brim with meat, potatoes, and onion? Now, that would keep me going, and the Grey Wardens certainly seem to agree! While the original recipe produces a much tougher pastry—mostly to keep the whole thing from falling apart in one's pack—another variation, championed by newer recruits from Orlais, incorporates the far more delicate Orlesian puff pastry. Whether eaten hot or cold, the results are certainly delicious, but I wouldn't recommend storing these pastries anywhere they might be jostled. Otherwise, you might open your pack to find a mess in place of a meal!

Contributor	Yield	Cook time	Difficulty
EMILY TAYLOR, SENIOR GAME DESIGNER	8 PASTRIES	60 TO 70 MINUTES (INCLUDING BAKING)	AVERAGE

Ingredients

Dough
Scant 2 cups flour

1 teaspoon salt

¾ cup (1½ sticks) cold butter

Filling
18 ounces lean ground beef

1 medium potato, diced

1 medium onion, diced

1 tablespoon salt

1 Sift the flour and salt into a bowl. Add the cold butter, and use two small sharp knives to cut it into pea-size lumps. Add just enough cold water that you can work the ingredients (still using the knife) into a dough firm enough to roll out.

2 Use a rolling pin to roll out the dough as flat as possible. Then fold the sides in toward the middle, fold again, and refrigerate for a few minutes.

3 Meanwhile, prepare the filling. Put the ground beef in a large mixing bowl. Add the potato, onion, and salt, and combine.

4 Preheat the oven to 400°F. Line a baking sheet with parchment paper.

5 Roll out the chilled dough as flat as possible, and use a small sharp knife to trace the edge of a small plate or bowl to form circles about 4¾ to 6 inches in size. Make sure that the dough stays as cool as possible in the process, and be sure not to pull or stretch it.

6 Arrange the dough circles evenly on the baking sheet, and set 1 to 2 tablespoons of the meat mixture in the center of each circle. Moisten the edges of the dough with a bit of water, and fold inward around the sides, then press the "seams" firmly together with your fingertips to seal the pockets. Use a sharp knife to make a small cut on each side so the steam generated during baking can escape.

7 Bake in the preheated oven for 30 to 40 minutes or until the dough begins to brown. Then remove the pastries, and set them on a cooling rack for several minutes to cool. Either enjoy them while still warm or add them to your provisions and take them along on patrol.

Pickled Eggs

Got a fever? A cold? An aching shoulder, perhaps? Ask any Fereldan for advice, and they'll be quick to prescribe you a pickled egg, the Fereldan cure for . . . well, pretty much anything! Actually, no, I take it back. You don't even have to ask. Looking a bit under the weather is prompt enough for most Fereldans to unleash a deluge of eggs, which is exactly what Commander Cullen found waiting for him in his office during the worst of his lyrium withdrawals. Whether the eggs really work is a completely different story, but I'd be the last person to complain if one was offered to me. I am Fereldan, after all. Still, next time you feel a bit of illness coming on, try one of these salty-sour eggs. You never know; it might actually work. And at the very least, you'll have the opportunity to enjoy one of Ferelden's finest snacks!

Yield	Cook time	Difficulty
10 PICKLED EGGS	40 MINUTES (PLUS AT LEAST 3 DAYS FOR FLAVORS TO MELD)	EASY

Ingredients

1 onion, cut in half

2 bay leaves

1 teaspoon allspice berries

2 whole cloves

1 tablespoon mustard seed

1 tablespoon peppercorns

1 small dried chili pepper

½ teaspoon caraway

1 quart (32 fluid ounces) water

2 tablespoons sugar

2 tablespoons salt

3 tablespoons white wine vinegar

10 eggs

Equipment

Preserving jar large enough to hold about 1½ quarts

1   Set the onion halves cut side down in a frying pan and caramelize without oil over medium heat until the cut sides are dark brown (about 3 to 4 minutes). Shortly before that happens, add the bay leaves, allspice, cloves, mustard seed, peppercorns, chili pepper, and caraway and combine. Briefly cook the seasonings with the onion until fragrant (about 2 to 3 minutes).

2   Transfer the seasonings to a pot and fill with a quart of water. Add the sugar, salt, and vinegar and bring to a boil over medium heat. Simmer gently, stirring occasionally, for 30 minutes.

3   Meanwhile, boil the eggs in a separate pot for 10 minutes. Drain, run the eggs under cold water, and tap them lightly so that the shell cracks slightly all around and the seasoning can soak into the eggs. Alternatively, you can shell the eggs entirely at this point.

4   Carefully transfer the eggs to a preserving jar large enough to hold everything, then pour in the hot broth and tightly seal the jar right away. Allow the eggs to cool completely at room temperature, then refrigerate the jars and allow them to stand for at least 3 days (ideally, longer—up to 7 days) so the flavors can meld.

5   The pickled eggs will keep for about 2 weeks in the refrigerator.

> This is a base recipe for pickled eggs. You can adjust it to your own tastes by adding other ingredients. For example, you can use different herbs and spices (such as rosemary, tarragon, dill, thyme, and curry) or aromatic ingredients, including beets, bell peppers, squash, and garlic.

Unidentified Meat

Have you ever heard a tale so exciting that you decide then and there that you absolutely have to see the truth of it for yourself? That was me when I learned about the mysterious, impossible-to-identify meat that's often served in taverns across Tevinter—usually with a heaping portion of Nevarran flat bread. Of course, sometimes, the truth is far less exciting. Because what did I find on my plate when I ordered a portion of this strange meat? Was it quillback? Dracolisk? Giant? No. It was chicken—chicken legs, to be precise. Ah, well. They were still delicious.

Yield	Cook time	Difficulty
4 SERVINGS	40 MINUTES	AVERAGE

Ingredients

2¼ pounds chicken legs

1 tablespoon dried sage

1 tablespoon dried rosemary

2 tablespoons dried thyme

2 tablespoons paprika

1 tablespoon salt

2 tablespoons chili flakes, plus more for sprinkling

7 tablespoons butter, cubed

1   Preheat the oven to 325°F. Position a rack in the middle of the oven. Place a large roasting pan containing an inch of water underneath the rack to catch any drippings.

2   Briefly rinse the chicken pieces in cold water, and pat dry with paper towels.

3   Combine the sage, rosemary, thyme, paprika, salt, and chili flakes in a small bowl.

4   Melt half the butter in the microwave, and combine with the seasonings to form a paste. Brush half the seasoning mixture onto the chicken legs on all sides, and set them on the oven rack. Cover loosely with aluminum foil and bake in the preheated oven for 30 minutes, turning the legs regularly and brushing with the seasoning mixture.

5   Remove the aluminum foil, brush the chicken legs on all sides with the remaining seasoning mixture, and increase the oven temperature to 425°F. Grill for another 4 to 5 minutes so the skin gets nice and crispy. Then remove the chicken from the oven, sprinkle with more chili flakes to taste (depending on how spicy you want the dish to be), and serve immediately.

Seheron Fish Pockets

Alas, for all of my desire to see every last bit of Thedas, there are still certain places where I simply cannot go. Take far-off Seheron, for example, a land that, according to the Hero of Ferelden's companion, Sten, smells like tea, incense, and the sea. Sounds lovely, no? What a shame, then, that all my knowledge comes secondhand—and this recipe is no exception.

I learned of this recipe from a member of the famous mercenary band Bull's Chargers. A group favorite, the fish is packed with flavor. On its own, this combination of spices might prove a bit too much for the more delicate Orlesian palates, but I find that the soft wrap and crisp vegetables temper the resultant heat a fair bit. Do note, however, that this dish has a tendency to fall apart if eaten haphazardly. I suppose that's why the mercenary who shared this recipe with me emphasized the importance of sitting down properly. He seemed to think that I might stand in my chair to eat it instead. Who does that?

Yield	Cook time	Difficulty
4 FISH POCKETS	25 MINUTES	AVERAGE

Ingredients

14 ounces pizza dough (store-bought)

14 ounces hot-smoked salmon fillet (store-bought)

½ bunch parsley, minced

1 shallot, minced

1 tablespoon salt

2 tablespoons coarse pepper, plus more for sprinkling

1 egg, beaten

1 Preheat the oven to 400°F. Line a baking sheet with parchment paper.

2 Use a rolling pin to roll out the pizza dough into a rectangle about ⅛ inch thick. Then use a small sharp knife or a pizza cutter to cut it into eight equal circles (about 4 inches in diameter).

3 Transfer the salmon to a bowl. Remove and dispose of the skin, if present. Finely shred the salmon with two forks. Add the parsley, shallot, salt, and pepper, then stir well to combine.

4 Place a quarter of the fish mixture in the center of each round of dough. Brush the edges of each round with a bit of beaten egg, and set a second round on top. Press the "seam" together with your fingers to close the pocket. Brush the top with the remaining egg, and sprinkle with coarse pepper to taste.

5 Set the pockets a couple inches apart on the baking sheet, and bake for about 15 minutes. If the dough begins to darken too much during baking, cover loosely with aluminum foil.

6 Remove the baking sheet from the oven, and allow the pockets to cool for 3 minutes. Then enjoy promptly.

Fereldan Hearty Scones

Traveling is tiring work, especially when circumstances beyond your control necessitate going by foot instead of by carriage. Thankfully, I had these hearty scones from home to keep me going! Unlike their sweeter, more delicate counterparts, Fereldan scones are packed with cheese and bacon, making them certain to keep you full until your next meal. Unfortunately, this also makes the scones a prime target for any nearby mabari, who love cheese and bacon as much as any other Fereldan. Don't make my mistake! Take a moment to survey your surroundings before enjoying your first bite; otherwise, a four-legged someone might do the honors for you.

Contributor	Yield	Cook time	Difficulty
HAREL EILAM, GAME ECONOMY DESIGNER	12 SCONES	30 MINUTES (INCLUDING BAKING)	AVERAGE

Ingredients

4 cups plus 2 tablespoons flour, plus more for the counter

5 teaspoons baking powder

1 teaspoon baking soda

1 teaspoon salt

7 teaspoons sugar

2 sticks plus 3 tablespoons cold butter, cut into small cubes

2 ounces Cheddar cheese, plus more for sprinkling

12 strips crispy bacon, crumbled

1½ cups buttermilk

1 egg

1 Preheat the oven to 350°F. Line a baking sheet with parchment paper.

2 Transfer the flour, baking powder, baking soda, salt, and sugar to a bowl, and combine thoroughly.

3 Add the butter, and stir well with a fork to combine.

4 Add the cheese, bacon, and buttermilk, then knead by hand until the mixture is just beginning to hold together as a loose dough.

5 Use a rolling pin to roll out the dough about 1 inch thick on a lightly floured surface. Cut into rough triangles with a small sharp knife, and set the pieces of dough on the baking sheet.

6 Beat the egg in a cup, and brush it over the tops of the scones. Sprinkle with cheese as desired.

7 Set the baking sheet in the oven, and bake for about 12 to 15 minutes or until the scones are firm. Remove the scones from the oven, and allow them to cool on the baking sheet for a few minutes before consuming.

Crow Feed

You don't see much rice outside of Antiva and its neighbor, Rivain. In fact, it's an especially rare sight in Ferelden, where any grain is seemingly always either barley or wheat. Evidently, very little of the rice Antiva produces ends up being exported, making it relatively cheap compared to other grains. It's no wonder, then, that rice is a key component in dishes favored by poorer Antivans. However, that doesn't make them any less delicious! Take crow feed, for example—a simple dish of rice, butter, and onions named after the (in)famous Antivan Crows. Although it's most certainly cheap, the taste is fit for a king!

Yield	Cook time	Difficulty
4 SERVINGS	30 MINUTES	EASY

Ingredients

Scant 3 tablespoons butter

2 large red onions, diced

7 ounces streaky bacon, coarsely chopped

14 ounces long-grain rice

3½ cups vegetable broth

Salt

Freshly ground black pepper

1 Add the butter to a medium pot and heat over medium heat. When the butter has melted, add the onions and bacon, and sweat until the onions are translucent on all sides (about 3 to 4 minutes). Add the rice, and pour the broth over it. Bring to a boil, stirring occasionally.

2 Reduce the heat to low; then cover and cook for 15 to 20 minutes or until the rice has absorbed nearly all the broth. Season to taste with salt and pepper.

Black Lichen Bread

No doubt your face is already creasing with trepidation. "But wait," you think, "isn't black lichen toxic?"

And yes. Yes, it is. But high temperatures seem to largely neutralize the lichen's toxicity, making it safe to consume. If you're still concerned, you can easily substitute any surface varieties for the lichen used in this recipe. Just make sure to thoroughly dry it, as you would with any lichen from underground. You can also use bark in place of lichen, but I think that defeats the point. This is supposed to be lichen bread, after all, not bark bread!

Yield	Cook time	Difficulty
1 LOAF	2 HOURS (INCLUDING STANDING AND BAKING)	AVERAGE

Ingredients

4 cups plus 2 tablespoons flour, plus more for the counter

8 grams activated charcoal powder

1½ teaspoons salt

1.5 ounces fresh yeast

1⅓ cups lukewarm water

1½ tablespoons butter, softened

Equipment

Loaf pan (about 3½ by 10 inches)

1   Sift the flour and charcoal powder into a large oven-safe mixing bowl. Add the salt, and combine thoroughly.

2   Transfer the yeast and water to a small bowl, and stir with a fork until the yeast has dissolved completely. Add to the mixing bowl with the butter, and knead with an electric mixer with the kneading hook attachment until a smooth dough forms (about 5 minutes); start on the lowest level, and gradually increase the speed to the highest setting.

3   Preheat the oven to 125°F, and then turn it off. Cover the bowl with a clean dish towel, and set it inside the warm oven to rise for about 25 to 30 minutes or until the dough has significantly increased in bulk.

4   Transfer the dough to a lightly floured surface, and knead by hand for about 2 to 3 minutes. Shape the dough into a loaf, and set it inside a loaf pan lined with parchment paper. Allow the dough to rise for another 30 minutes or until it has once again grown significantly in bulk.

5   Toward the end of the rising time, preheat the oven to 425°F. Set a small oven-safe bowl of water on the base of the oven or on a rack underneath the loaf, depending on your style of oven.

6   Bake the bread on the center rack for about 40 minutes. Remove it from the oven, cover with a clean dish towel, and allow to cool completely in the pan. Carefully turn the loaf out of the pan when you're ready to slice it.

Hearth Cakes

Some lovely comfort food, courtesy of the Dalish. These cakes are traditionally made over the hearth on an iron griddle or skillet (hence the name). While the original recipe calls for halla butter, I've found that other types of butter work just as well. The resulting dough stays moist on the inside, but crisp and flaky on the outside. In other words: perfect.

Although hearth cakes can be made plain, I recommend adding some dried fruit into the mix. Cranberries, raisins, and currants all work. I believe the Dalish simply use whatever is on hand. Of course, if you're feeling a bit mischievous, you could mix in some hot peppers instead: Just be prepared to be cursed as loudly and vehemently as Fen'Harel, the Lord of Tricksters himself!

Yield	Cook time	Difficulty
2 HEARTH CAKES	1 HOUR 40 MINUTES (INCLUDING STANDING AND BAKING)	AVERAGE

Ingredients

4 cups plus 2 tablespoons flour, plus more for the counter

3 tablespoons fresh yeast

¼ cup sugar

6 tablespoons butter, softened

1 teaspoon vanilla extract

½ teaspoon salt

1 cup plus 2 tablespoons lukewarm milk

7 ounces dried cranberries

1 tablespoon vegetable oil

Equipment

2 clean aluminum cans
(each with a capacity of about 20 fluid ounces)

1   Sift the flour into a medium bowl, and use a tablespoon to form a small hollow in the middle. Crumble the yeast into the hollow with your fingers. Add the sugar, butter, vanilla extract, salt, and milk. Knead with an electric mixer until you have a firm but smooth dough and can hardly see any flour (about 3 to 4 minutes).

2   Cover the dough with a clean towel, and allow to rise in a warm place for 30 minutes. Alternatively, preheat the oven to 125°F, then turn it off and set the covered bowl inside the oven for the same amount of time.

3   After the rising time, set the dough on a lightly floured surface. Press down a bit with your hands, and sprinkle the cranberries over the top. Knead thoroughly to evenly distribute the cranberries throughout the dough. Then use a knife to cut the dough in half down the middle.

4   Use kitchen scissors to cut parchment paper to fit inside the aluminum cans. Brush the bottom of each can with a bit of oil. Then insert the parchment paper seamlessly into the cans, and place each half of the dough in one can. Press the dough into place so the cans are completely filled. Cover with a clean dish cloth, and allow the dough to rise for another 20 minutes.

5   Shortly before the end of the rising time, preheat the oven to 350°F. Set the cans inside and bake for 30 minutes until the dough is golden brown. Remove the cans from the oven, and allow to rest for a few minutes before carefully turning the cakes out of the cans. It should be easy to do this, but be careful so you don't burn your fingers!

Peasant Bread

While traveling through Orlais, I spied this rustic and hearty bread being eaten by both Dalish and city elves alike. The recipe is very straightforward, calling for wheat, salt, and grease in nearly equal parts, and it produces a biscuit that feels like it would be right at home in any Fereldan dish. It does a wonderful job of mopping up any last bits of stew left inside your bowl, but it also pairs well with a bit of butter and jam.

Yield	Cook time	Difficulty
ABOUT 12 ROLLS	ABOUT 3 HOURS (INCLUDING RISING AND BAKING)	AVERAGE

Ingredients

1 package active dry yeast

4 cups plus 2 tablespoons flour, plus more for your hands

1 level teaspoon salt

⅓ cup sugar

1 cup plus 2 tablespoons lukewarm milk

2 egg yolks

5 tablespoons butter, melted

1 Combine the yeast, flour, salt, and sugar in a bowl and stir with a tablespoon. Then add the milk, egg yolks, and butter and knead with a stand mixer or an electric mixer with the kneading hook attachment until all the ingredients have combined and the dough pulls away from the sides of the bowl on its own (about 5 to 6 minutes).

2 Shape the dough into a ball with your hands, then return it to the bowl. Cover the bowl with a clean dish towel and allow it to stand in a warm place for 1 hour.

3 Line a baking sheet with parchment paper.

4 Knead the dough firmly and thoroughly in the bowl. If it is too sticky, lightly flour your hands. Then divide the dough into 12 approximately equal servings and roughly shape them into rolls. Set them on the baking sheet about 1 inch apart. Cover with a clean dish towel and allow to rise for another hour.

5 Toward the end of the rising time, preheat the oven to 400°F.

6 Bake the rolls for about 30 minutes until golden brown.

Soups & Stews

Merrill's Blood Soup

In the same vein as Llomerryn red, this is not actually blood—it's just red. The color comes from the beetroot, which gives the soup a rich, earthy flavor that goes well with the roasted chickpeas sprinkled on top. Some might find the vibrant crimson hue off-putting, in the same way that many shun the practice of blood magic. However, as mages like Merrill have shown, I think it's best to not judge by appearances or by what you think you know. Take the time to experience things for yourself, and you might find yourself pleasantly surprised!

Yield	*Cook time*	*Difficulty*
4 SERVINGS	40 TO 50 MINUTES	AVERAGE

Ingredients

Masala-Seasoned Chickpeas

7 ounces canned chickpeas, drained

1 tablespoon olive oil

1 tablespoon sea salt

1 tablespoon garam masala

Blood Soup

1 tablespoon vegetable oil

1 red onion, diced

1 piece fresh ginger root (about 2 inches), minced

1 garlic clove, minced

1 pound potatoes, peeled and diced

18 ounces red beets (from a jar or can), diced

1 quart (32 fluid ounces) vegetable broth

Salt

Pepper

1 to 2 teaspoons agave syrup

5 fluid ounces coconut milk

1 teaspoon horseradish

Fresh cilantro, finely chopped, for garnishing

Equipment

Freezer bag

Immersion blender

To make the masala-seasoned chickpeas:

1. Start by preparing the chickpeas. Preheat the oven to 400°F. Line a baking sheet with parchment paper. Pat the drained chickpeas dry with paper towels.

2. Transfer the olive oil and chickpeas to a freezer bag. Seal tightly, and shake so the chickpeas are coated with oil. Spread in an even layer over the baking sheet and roast for about 35 to 45 minutes until crisp, turning every 10 minutes so they do not burn.

3. While the chickpeas are in the oven, begin preparing the blood soup.

To make the blood soup:

4. Heat the vegetable oil in a large pot over medium heat. Add the onion and sweat, stirring occasionally, until translucent (about 2 to 3 minutes). Add the ginger and garlic and sauté together for 1 minute. Then add the potatoes and sauté briefly (2 to 3 minutes).

5. Add the beets to the pot, then add the vegetable broth. Season to taste with salt and pepper, bring to a boil, and then simmer, covered, for about 20 to 25 minutes or until the vegetables are cooked. Add the agave syrup and coconut milk, then use an immersion blender to purée coarsely in the pot. Stir in the horseradish and season to taste with salt and pepper.

6. Transfer the roasted chickpeas to a medium bowl. Sprinkle with sea salt and garam masala, and combine thoroughly so the chickpeas are coated all over with seasoning. Allow to cool for several minutes before serving. Store in an airtight sealed container until consumed.

7. Divide the soup among four serving bowls, sprinkle to taste with masala-seasoned chickpeas, and serve garnished with a bit of freshly chopped cilantro.

Fereldan Potato and Leek Soup

Most people immediately think of Orlais when it comes to creamy soups, and I can't blame them. However, as often as cream might appear in their cuisine, the Orlesians certainly don't have a monopoly on it, whether in soup or otherwise! This dish is 100% Fereldan through and through, and the recipe I've noted here is actually Mum's. Of course, I couldn't help but put my own little twist on it. Instead of using a side of toasted bread to give the meal that necessary bit of crunch, I turned my attention abroad, settling on chickpeas from Rivain, toasted to crouton-like crispiness. In a way, this recipe is very much a reflection of me, now that my journey is coming to an end. While my origins are unmistakably Fereldan, my travels across Thedas have touched me in a lasting way, and I am all the richer for it.

Yield	Cook time	Difficulty
4 SERVINGS	35 MINUTES	AVERAGE

Ingredients

3 tablespoons vegetable oil

1 onion, diced

5 ounces bacon, coarsely chopped

18 ounces leeks, sliced into thin rings

14 ounces potatoes, peeled and coarsely diced

½ bunch soup vegetables, diced

⅔ cup dry white wine

25 fluid ounces vegetable broth

1 teaspoon salt

1 teaspoon pepper

1 teaspoon oregano

1 teaspoon nutmeg

Roasted chickpeas, store-bought, for garnishing

Fresh parsley, finely chopped, for garnishing

1. Heat the oil in a large pot over medium heat. Add the onion and sweat until translucent (about 2 minutes). Add the bacon and sauté (about 2 minutes). Add the leek, potatoes, and soup vegetables to the pot and brown on all sides (about 2 to 3 minutes). Deglaze with the white wine, pour in the vegetable broth, and simmer, stirring occasionally, for about 20 to 25 minutes or until the potatoes are done.

2. Season to taste with salt, pepper, oregano, and nutmeg.

3. Divide among four bowls, garnish as desired with chickpeas, and serve sprinkled with a bit of freshly chopped parsley.

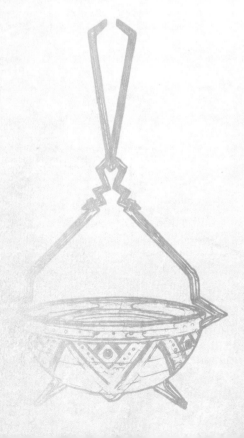

The Hanged Man's Mystery Meat Stew

A famous dish from the Hanged Man tavern in Kirkwall—or infamous, I suppose, depending on your perspective. Personally, after having heard so much about it, I couldn't wait to taste it, even if the establishment, as Fenris once so succinctly put it, smelled of sour ale, vomit, and desperation. Oh, yes. I can hear what you're thinking. A Fereldan excited about yet another stew. How predictable. But this is the tavern's feature dish! Why shouldn't I be excited? It's made from a different meat every morning. I suspect mine was pork, although after overhearing the waitress tell another patron that they hang people who ask stupid questions from the rafters, I declined to confirm.

Yield	Cook time	Difficulty
6 SERVINGS	40 MINUTES	AVERAGE

Ingredients

1 tablespoon olive oil

1 large onion, diced

1 garlic clove, minced

3.5 ounces pancetta

21 ounces ground pork

2 tablespoons tomato paste

¾ cup plus 2 tablespoons dry red wine

14 ounces canned kidney beans, drained

10.5 ounces canned diced tomatoes

5.3 ounces canned corn, drained

1 red bell pepper, coarsely chopped

1 red chili pepper, minced

2 bay leaves

3 to 4 whole allspice berries

1 whole clove

Salt

Pepper

Paprika

Caraway

Oregano

Pinch of sugar

Squeeze of lemon

Fresh parsley, finely chopped, for garnishing

1 Heat the olive oil in a large pot over medium heat. Add the onion and garlic and sweat until translucent (about 2 to 3 minutes). Add the pancetta and sweat (about 1 to 2 minutes). Add the ground pork, and sauté until the meat is lightly browned on all sides but not too dark (about 5 to 6 minutes). Stir in the tomato paste and continue to cook briefly. Deglaze with the red wine.

2 Add the kidney beans, tomatoes, corn, bell pepper, chili pepper, bay leaves, allspice, and clove to the pot. Stir well to combine, and simmer, stirring occasionally, for 20 minutes or until the dish has thickened noticeably (but not too thick).

3 Season to taste with salt, pepper, paprika, caraway, and oregano. Stir in a pinch of sugar and a squeeze of lemon. Simmer for another 2 to 3 minutes, then remove from heat. Remove the clove, allspice, and bay leaves, and dispose of them. Allow the stew to stand for 5 minutes.

4 Serve garnished with a bit of freshly chopped parsley.

Fish Chowder

As Antivan as it gets! A bowl of this thick, creamy soup will have you feeling like you're in Antiva City. No need for any pickpockets, corrupt politicians, or Antivan leather to further enhance the experience—the word "enhance" being entirely debatable, of course. I can't imagine that the smell of rotting flesh would do much for anyone's appetite, although Zevran Arainai might disagree with me on that. Evidently, becoming an accomplished assassin can have a pronounced effect on one's tastes. But if you ask me, this desire for rather unusual accompaniments is likely born of something much more universally understood: homesickness.

Yield	Cook time	Difficulty
5 TO 6 SERVINGS	40 MINUTES	AVERAGE

Ingredients

2 tablespoons olive oil

2 shallots, minced

1 garlic clove, minced

1 celery rib, thinly sliced

½ leek, sliced into thin rings

½ green bell pepper, thinly sliced into strips

½ red bell pepper, thinly sliced into strips

3.5 ounces corn (canned), drained

1 red chili, sliced into thin rings

10.5 ounces potatoes (russet or similar), peeled and quartered

Pinch of salt, plus more to taste

Pinch of pepper, plus more to taste

⅔ cup dry white wine

17 fluid ounces fish broth

17 fluid ounces vegetable broth

1 teaspoon saffron

10.5 ounces frozen prawns (ready to cook), thawed

14 ounces fish fillets (cod, for example), cut into bite-size pieces

¾ cup plus 2 tablespoons cream

2 egg yolks

Juice and zest of ½ lemon

Fresh parsley, finely chopped, for garnishing

Equipment

Immersion blender

1   Heat the olive oil in a large pot over medium heat. Add the shallot and garlic and sweat until translucent (2 to 3 minutes). Add the celery, leek, bell peppers, corn, and chili; stir to combine, and cook for 2 to 3 minutes more. Add the potatoes. Season with salt and pepper, and then deglaze with white wine. Bring to a brief boil, add the two kinds of broth and saffron, and simmer for 10 minutes, stirring occasionally.

2   Remove two ladles' worth of broth and vegetables to a blender and purée finely.

3   Add the prawns and fish fillets to the soup. Reduce the heat to low and cook for another 10 minutes for the flavors to meld.

4   Whip the cream and egg yolks with the vegetable purée in a mixing cup or bowl. Add to the soup. Stir well to combine, and increase the heat back to medium. Simmer for 5 minutes. Season with the lemon juice and zest, and add more salt and pepper as needed.

5   Serve with a bit of freshly chopped parsley.

Sweet and Sour Cabbage Soup

This Fereldan staple is often more solid than liquid, filled to the brim with cabbage, tomatoes, and other vegetables. Paired with a thick slice of dark bread, it makes for a filling and satisfying meal, one guaranteed to leave you full of warmth for hours afterward on even the coldest of days. A perfect fit for us Fereldans, you might think, but we aren't the only ones who enjoy this soup on the regular.

Apparently, there's a troupe of actors in Orlais whose sole focus is a popular comedy set in the fictional Fereldan village of Wilkshire Downs. Unfortunately, I wasn't able to see it for myself, as the performance sold out almost instantly. But in order to play their roles most convincingly, the actors went so far as to change their diets to match those of their characters. For example, there's a mayor who specifically eats cabbage soup. Personally, I don't think I'd enjoy subsisting only on cabbage soup for an extended period of time, but you can't help but applaud them for their dedication to their craft!

Yield	Cook time	Difficulty
6 SERVINGS	60 MINUTES	AVERAGE

Ingredients

1 medium head of cabbage

9 ounces carrots, coarsely chopped

1 celery rib, coarsely chopped

5.3 ounces canned diced tomatoes

½ red chili pepper, coarsely chopped

1 tablespoon olive oil

5 onions, diced

¼ red bell pepper, diced

¼ yellow bell pepper, diced

¼ green bell pepper, diced

2 to 3 medium pickles, thinly sliced

1 quart (32 fluid ounces) vegetable broth

⅓ cup plus 2 tablespoons pickle juice (from the pickle jar)

2 quarts (64 fluid ounces) water

2 tablespoons bouillon powder

Salt

Pepper

Fresh parsley, for garnishing

1 Wash the cabbage, remove the core with a large sharp knife, and cut the cabbage in half. Then cut the halves in half again, and slice the quarters into thin strips (about ⅜ to ¾ inch thick).

2 Finely purée the carrots, celery, tomatoes, and chili pepper with a food processor or immersion blender.

3 Add the olive oil to a large pot, and heat over medium heat. Sweat the onion until translucent (about 2 to 3 minutes). Add the bell peppers and sauté briefly (about 1 to 2 minutes). Add the carrot-tomato purée and the pickles and stir well to combine. Pour in the vegetable broth, pickle juice, and water. Add the bouillon powder and simmer, stirring occasionally, for 40 minutes or until the cabbage is tender. Season to taste with salt and pepper.

4 Serve garnished with a bit of fresh parsley.

Lentil Soup

Lentils and onions—open any pantry across Thedas, and I'm certain you'll find these two ingredients sitting on the shelves. They're both relatively inexpensive and keep well for an extended period of time. Best of all, they go with pretty much anything! Still, I couldn't help but wonder what it would be like if these two Thedosian staples played a starring role instead of a supporting one. So I combined a recipe that's popular in elven alienages with some classic Tevinter flavors to supply an answer to this question. And what a delicious answer it is!

Yield	Cook time	Difficulty
4 SERVINGS	50 MINUTES	AVERAGE

Ingredients

1 bunch soup vegetables (such as carrots, celery, leek, parsley)

2 tablespoons olive oil

1 onion, diced

5.3 ounces pancetta

3 potatoes, peeled and coarsely cubed

7 ounces common brown lentils

1 quart (32 fluid ounces) vegetable broth

¼ teaspoon cumin

1 teaspoon sugar

3 teaspoons white wine vinegar

Salt

Pepper

Fresh watercress, for garnishing

1 Wash the vegetables. Slice the leek into thin rings. Peel and dice the carrots and celery root.

2 Heat the oil in a medium pot over medium heat. Add the onion, and sweat until translucent (about 2 to 3 minutes). Add the pancetta, and sweat briefly (about 2 minutes). Add the prepared soup vegetables, and brown on all sides (about 3 to 4 minutes). Add the potatoes and lentils to the pot. Pour the vegetable broth over the rest of the ingredients. Cover and simmer, stirring occasionally, until the vegetables are done and the soup has taken on a certain thick consistency (about 25 to 30 minutes).

3 Season to taste with cumin, sugar, vinegar, salt, and pepper. Serve garnished with a bit of fresh watercress.

Like all soups of its kind, this soup tastes even better if given time for the flavors to meld. Feel free to make it the day before you plan to serve it!

Nettle Soup

I first encountered nettles as a child, when I tripped and fell face-first in a whole patch of them. Many tears were shed, along with a lecture from Mum to play elsewhere from now on. In short, it was far from a pleasant experience. So I was understandably dubious when confronted with the idea of using nettles as an ingredient in my cooking. How could something so painful to the touch be in any way edible, let alone pleasant on the tongue?

Funnily enough, I didn't even have to taste it to understand. Though I doubt she'd appreciate it, I immediately thought of Lady Morrigan. She is, in a word, prickly, much like a nettle. And yet, despite her oftentimes cruel manner, no one can deny that she's done much for Thedas's benefit, helping not just the Hero of Ferelden, but also the Inquisitor. She's a perfect example of how first impressions are not always the most correct.

So, yes, nettles are both incredibly nutritious and delicious, contrary to my expectations. Combine them with potatoes, stock, and a dollop of cream, and you'll have a soup so tasty you won't be able to stop yourself from licking the bowl clean!

Yield	Cook time	Difficulty
4 SERVINGS	45 MINUTES	AVERAGE

Ingredients

2 tablespoons vegetable oil

1 shallot, minced

1 garlic clove, minced

14 ounces nettles,
tips of leaves only, minced

1 leek, sliced into thin rings

1 large potato, diced

22 fluid ounces vegetable broth

⅓ cup plus 2 tablespoons
white wine

Pinch of salt

Pinch of nutmeg

Coconut milk, for garnishing

1 teaspoon multicolored
peppercorns, coarsely crushed

Equipment

Immersion blender

1. Transfer the vegetable oil to a medium pot and heat over medium heat. Add the shallot and garlic and sweat until translucent (about 2 to 3 minutes). Add the nettles and leek and cook until the nettles have wilted (about 5 to 6 minutes). Add the potatoes, then add the broth and wine and simmer, stirring occasionally, for 30 minutes.

2. Remove from heat and allow to cool briefly. Then purée very finely with an immersion blender and season with salt and nutmeg.

3. Divide among four deep plates or bowls, garnish each with a dollop of coconut milk, and serve sprinkled with ¼ teaspoon crushed multicolored peppercorns.

King Alistair's Lamb and Pea Stew

Hearty, humble, and straightforward to make—the three key aspects of any good Fereldan stew. This is a dish so ubiquitous that it's become almost synonymous with Fereldan cuisine in general. I'm certain you've heard many a clever quip about our stews, perhaps even from a Fereldan! But let me be the first to assure you that, no, contrary to what King Alistair may have said, we don't cook our ingredients until they're all "a uniform gray color." Throwing them into the largest pot we can find, on the other hand … that much is true. If you're going to make a stew, you might as well make a lot of it! Although Mum's stews will always rule my heart, I'd be lying if I said this recipe—its namesake's view on Fereldan stews aside—didn't come close to stealing the crown. (Sorry, Mum!)

Yield	Cook time	Difficulty
4 TO 5 SERVINGS	60 MINUTES	AVERAGE

Ingredients

Salt

25 ounces potatoes
(russet or similar),
peeled and coarsely diced

1 tablespoon oil

2 onions, diced

18 ounces ground lamb

1 tablespoon tomato paste

5 fluid ounces beef stock

5.3 ounces canned peas
and carrots, drained

Freshly ground black pepper

1 tablespoon paprika

6 tablespoons butter, cubed,
plus more to grease the pan

⅓ cup plus 2 tablespoons cream

Generous pinch of nutmeg

5.3 ounces cheese,
grated or shredded

2 sprigs thyme, with the
leaves plucked off

Equipment

Potato masher

Casserole dish
(about 6¼ by 10½ inches)

1 Generously salt a large pot of water and place it over medium heat. Add the potatoes and cook for 20 minutes or until the potatoes are cooked and tender.

2 Meanwhile, heat the oil in a frying pan over medium heat. Add the onion and sweat until translucent (about 2 to 3 minutes). Add the ground lamb and sauté until the meat is brown and crumbly. Stir in the tomato paste and continue to cook briefly. Deglaze with the beef stock, then add the peas and carrots. Stir well to combine, then season to taste with salt, pepper, and paprika. Simmer, uncovered, for 10 minutes, stirring constantly.

3 Preheat the oven to 350°F.

4 Carefully drain the potatoes and return them to the pot. Add the butter and mash the potatoes as finely as possible with a potato masher. Add the cream and season generously with pepper, salt, and nutmeg. Stir until creamy.

5 Grease the casserole dish. Add the meat-and-vegetable mixture and spread it in the pan. Top with an even layer of mashed potatoes and smooth the top. Sprinkle with the cheese and thyme and bake for about 15 minutes or until the cheese has melted.

6 Remove the pan from the oven, allow to cool briefly, and serve promptly.

Main Courses

Stuffed Cabbage

Gathering is just as important as hunting for the Avvar. It's like Mum said: You can't live off only meat, and any meal without vegetables is a meal half-finished. Of course, I didn't understand her reasoning as a child, especially one who was single-handedly waging a war against the green menace on my plate. But now that I'm older, I have a new appreciation for her words. Plus, with a bit of proper seasoning, and some meat, even the most unappealing of vegetables can be delicious.

Yield	Cook time	Difficulty
5 TO 6 SERVINGS	1 HOUR 20 MINUTES	AVERAGE

Ingredients

Cabbage
1 large head of cabbage
3 tablespoons bread crumbs
18 ounces ground meat
2 red onions, diced
1 egg
Pinch of salt
Pinch of pepper
Pinch of grated nutmeg

Sauce
1 tablespoon olive oil
2 red onions, coarsely chopped
1 carrot, coarsely chopped
1 leek, coarsely chopped
½ celery root (celeriac), coarsely chopped
2 tablespoons tomato paste
⅓ cup dry red wine
1 cup plus 2 tablespoons water
Salt
Pepper

Equipment
Casserole dish
(about 8½ by 11 inches)

1. Wash the cabbage, and pat dry with paper towels. Use a small sharp knife to remove the outer leaves and cut out the core. Carefully hollow out the cabbage so that the sides remain intact and about 2 inches thick.

2. Preheat the oven to 400°F.

3. Put the bread crumbs, ground meat, onions, and egg in a bowl, and combine well with your hands. Season to taste with salt, pepper, and nutmeg.

4. Fill the hollowed-out cabbage with the ground meat mixture. Set it in the casserole dish, opening side up, and cook for 15 minutes.

5. Meanwhile, prepare the sauce. Heat the olive oil in a frying pan over medium heat. Add the onion and sweat until translucent (about 2 to 3 minutes). Add the carrot, leek, and celery root and sauté on all sides (about 3 to 4 minutes). Stir in the tomato paste and cook all the ingredients together briefly (1 minute). Deglaze with the red wine, and then reduce. When nearly all the liquid has evaporated, fill the pan with the water and season to taste with salt and pepper.

6. Pour the vegetables and liquid over the precooked cabbage. Loosely cover the casserole dish with aluminum foil, lower the oven temperature to 365°F, and bake for 45 minutes.

7. After the end of the baking time, set the cabbage on a large serving plate. Strain the sauce and pour it over the inside of the cabbage. Use a large sharp knife to cut the cabbage into further servings at the table. This dish is excellent with salted or mashed potatoes.

Antivan Gnocchi

Phew! Antivan meals sure are something to behold—and, to think, for Antivan nobles like Lady Josephine, these decadent spreads are just another dinner! Every time I thought we'd reached the last course, another was swiftly brought out. After ten dishes full of ingredients like olives, truffles, pasta, and cream, it's a wonder I didn't have to be rolled away from the table! In retrospect, I probably overindulged in the gnocchi, which were dressed with leeks and a rich cheese sauce. While they're delicious, these small lumps of wheat flour, egg, salt, and potato are incredibly filling. Still, I cannot say I won't repeat this mistake next time I find myself at an Antivan table—nor will I regret it if I do!

Yield	Cook time	Difficulty
4 SERVINGS	45 MINUTES	AVERAGE

Ingredients

Wild Garlic Gnocchi

Salt

21 ounces potatoes
(russet or similar)

1 ounce wild garlic (leaves only)

1 egg

3 tablespoons flour

2 tablespoons semolina,
finely ground

Basil Pesto

0.88 ounce pine nuts,
plus more for garnishing

2 garlic cloves, minced

3 bunches fresh basil
(about 1 to 1.4 ounces),
washed and drained

Pinch of salt,
plus more as needed

3 ounces Parmesan,
plus more for garnishing

½ cup plus 2 tablespoons
olive oil

Pinch of pepper

Equipment

Immersion blender

Potato ricer

Mortar and pestle

To make the wild garlic gnocchi:

1 Generously salt a medium pot of water and bring to a boil over medium heat. Add the potatoes and cook for 25 minutes or until the potatoes are tender.

2 Meanwhile, wash the ramson (wild garlic) leaves, shake dry, and cut into strips. Transfer the leaves to a mixing cup or bowl and add the egg; purée very finely using the immersion blender.

3 Drain the potatoes and allow them to cool for several minutes until you can work with them without burning your fingers. Then pass them through a potato ricer into a bowl. Add the wild garlic mixture, flour, and semolina and generously season with salt. Knead thoroughly to combine.

4 Shape the potato dough into rolls about 1 inch wide and cut them into pieces about ¾ inch long. Press flat lightly, and use a fork to create a decorative pattern, as desired.

To make the basil pesto:

5 Heat a dry frying pan over medium heat. Add the pine nuts and toast on all sides (about 2 to 3 minutes). Remove the pine nuts from the pan and allow them to cool briefly (2 to 3 minutes).

6 Transfer the still-warm pine nuts and garlic to the mortar and crush until you have a smooth cream. Add the basil and salt and crush thoroughly until you have a smooth green to light green mass. Add the Parmesan and olive oil and thoroughly stir or crush again to form a creamy paste. Season to taste with pepper and possibly a bit more salt.

7 Generously salt a large pot of water and bring to a boil over medium heat. Add the gnocchi and cook for about 3 to 4 minutes. Then remove the gnocchi and allow it to drain thoroughly in a strainer. Return the gnocchi to the pot, and gently mix it with the basil pesto.

8 Divide the gnocchi among four deep plates or bowls, garnish each with toasted pine nuts, and sprinkle with a bit of freshly grated Parmesan. Serve immediately.

Antivan Paella

Bordered by the Rialto Bay to the east, Antiva is populated mostly on the coast. It's no wonder, then, that seafood plays a starring role in Antivan cuisine. There's no dish that exemplifies this more than the classic Antivan paella. Rice, saffron, and a variety of seafood (from whole shrimp to cuttlefish to mussels) come together to create an aromatic smorgasbord of everything the ocean has to offer. Best of all, it's all made in a single pot—truly a dish after my own stew-loving Fereldan heart, if King Alistair's thoughts on Fereldan cuisine are to be believed! Although paella is traditionally cooked in a shallow, wide pan called a paellera (or, more confusingly, a paella in certain regions of Antiva), it can be prepared in virtually any deep skillet. Be sure to pair your paella with a glass of wine—ideally, an Antivan vintage, according to Lady Josephine, whose opinion on such matters can certainly be trusted—for the full experience.

Yield	Cook time	Difficulty
4 SERVINGS	50 MINUTES	AVERAGE

Ingredients

3 tablespoons olive oil, divided

14 ounces chicken breast fillet, cut into bite-size pieces

1 teaspoon salt, plus more as needed

1 teaspoon pepper, plus more as needed

1 teaspoon paprika

½ red bell pepper, cored and thinly sliced into strips

½ green bell pepper, cored and thinly sliced into strips

1 large onion, diced

3 garlic cloves, minced

3.5 ounces canned tomato purée

8.8 ounces paella or risotto rice (uncooked)

3½ cups chicken or poultry stock

½ teaspoon saffron threads

12 ounces mixed frozen seafood, thawed (such as mussels, squid rings, and shrimp)

10.5 ounces king prawns (fresh or frozen)

3.5 ounces frozen peas

1 sprig rosemary, with the leaves plucked off

2 bay leaves

1 tablespoon lemon juice

Fresh parsley, minced

1 Preheat the oven to 425°F.

2 Heat 1 tablespoon olive oil in a large, deep oven-safe frying pan over high heat. Add the chicken; season with the salt, pepper, and paprika and brown on all sides (about 2 to 3 minutes). Add both kinds of bell peppers and cook all ingredients together for 2 minutes. Remove the mixture from the pan and set aside.

3 Heat the remaining olive oil in the pan. Add the onion and garlic and sweat until translucent and fragrant (about 2 to 3 minutes). Add the tomato purée and rice and stir well to combine. Deglaze with the stock. Add the saffron; bring to a brief boil, stirring occasionally, then set the entire pan, uncovered, on the middle rack of the oven. Bake for 20 minutes.

4 When the time is up, carefully remove the pan from the oven and stir in the seafood (including the king prawns), along with the peas, rosemary, bay leaves, chicken, and bell pepper. Stir well to combine. Then set the pan back in the oven, uncovered, for another 15 minutes.

5 Remove the paella from the oven, season to taste with pepper and salt, and drizzle evenly with the lemon juice. To serve, sprinkle with chopped fresh parsley and enjoy.

Grilled Poussin

The Chasind sure love their poussin. And who can blame them? I love it, too! It's a great alternative to the roasted turkey one might normally trot out for guests—although, I admit, the length of the guest list will likely be the deciding factor here. A poussin is a significantly smaller bird, after all, and as much as we might love the kitchen, sometimes we must be economical in our choices. Still, for a more intimate dinner party, you can't go wrong with this dish!

Although the Chasind typically cook poussin in a single large pot over an open fire for an extended period of time, a similar effect can be achieved with any other cookware of suitable size and an oven. Marinating and basting the meat keep it moist. That's the secret to a meat so tender that it practically falls off the bone!

Yield	Cook time	Difficulty
4 SERVINGS	3 HOURS (INCLUDING MARINATING AND COOKING)	AVERAGE

Ingredients

2 poussins (spring chickens), each about 18 ounces, ready to cook

1 lemon

1 garlic clove, minced

3 sprigs thyme, leaves only

6 tablespoons olive oil

2 tablespoons honey

Pinch of pepper

3 tablespoons teriyaki sauce

2 tablespoons soy sauce

1 teaspoon sriracha sauce

2 tablespoons smoked paprika

Equipment

Juicer

Zester or kitchen grater

Freezer bag

Casserole dish (about 8½ by 11 inches)

1 Rinse the poussins in cold water and pat dry with paper towels. Transfer them to a large freezer bag.

2 Rinse the lemon in hot water, pat dry with paper towels, and then zest and juice.

3 Combine the lemon juice, garlic, thyme, olive oil, honey, pepper, teriyaki sauce, soy sauce, sriracha sauce, and paprika in a small bowl. Pour the mixture into the bag with the poussins. Seal, then gently massage the marinade into the poussins. Refrigerate for 2 hours to marinate.

4 Remove the poussins from the refrigerator and allow them to stand at room temperature for 15 minutes.

5 Meanwhile, preheat the oven to 400°F.

6 Transfer the poussins and the marinade to the casserole dish and bake on the middle rack for 30 minutes until golden brown. Meanwhile, pour the drippings that collect in the pan over the poussins regularly (every 10 minutes). Then turn the broiler to high for about 3 to 4 minutes, until the skin is nice and crispy.

7 Remove the poussins from the oven and briefly set them on a plate lined with paper towels to drain (about 2 to 3 minutes). Serve promptly.

Gurgut Roast with Lowlander Spices and Mushroom Sauce

It was spring when I trudged through the Frostbacks on my way toward one of the many Avvar settlements that populate the area. As this is the time of year when the Avvar begin preparing for the following winter by smoking meat, pickling vegetables, and drying fruit, I thought it an ideal time to visit and observe. Unfortunately, springtime is also the gurgut's mating season. As a result, I nearly discovered firsthand why travelers are advised to keep their distance from these brightly colored beasts.

Luckily, a nearby group of Avvar hunters quickly came to my aid, and I was spared the indignity of beating at the beast with a ladle. In an expression of my thanks, I shared with them several jars of spices from home, which they happily accepted. These Lowlander spices are prized among the Avvar and often reserved for feasts as rare delicacies. What unparalleled good fortune, then, that I later had the opportunity to dine on the slain gurgut, now roasted and seasoned with the spices I had gifted, at the hunters' hold.

Yield	Cook time	Difficulty
5 SERVINGS	1 HOUR 10 MINUTES (INCLUDING COOKING)	AVERAGE

Ingredients

1 teaspoon salt, plus more to taste

Pinch of pepper

1 pork roast (about 2½ pounds)

1 teaspoon paprika

2 tablespoons mustard

1 tablespoon lard

17 fluid ounces vegetable broth

1 tablespoon butter

2 onions, diced

2 garlic cloves, minced

3.5 ounces pancetta

1 ounce dried cranberries

18 ounces mixed mushrooms (such as crimini or porcini), thinly sliced or cut into bite-size pieces

⅓ cup plus 2 tablespoons white wine

2 tablespoons dried thyme

1 teaspoon cumin

⅔ cup cream

½ bunch fresh chives, thinly sliced

Equipment

Roasting pan

1. Preheat the oven to 350°F.

2. Salt and pepper the roast on all sides, and sprinkle with paprika. Brush the mustard over the meat.

3. Melt the lard in a large frying pan over high heat. Add the roast and brown on all sides (about 3 to 4 minutes). Set the roast in the roasting pan and bake for about 45 minutes, regularly turning and brushing with the pan drippings.

4. When the baking time is up, increase the oven temperature to 425°F and cook for another 10 minutes or until done.

5. While the roast is in the oven, melt the butter in a large frying pan over medium heat. Add the onion and garlic and sweat until translucent or fragrant (about 3 to 4 minutes). Add the pancetta and sweat (about 2 to 3 minutes). Add the cranberries and mushrooms and combine thoroughly. Cover and simmer, stirring occasionally, for 15 to 20 minutes or until the mushrooms have shrunk significantly and released their liquid. Then add the white wine and thyme, stir, and reduce the heat to low. Simmer for 5 minutes, then keep warm until the roast is done.

6. When the roast is done, transfer it from the roasting pan to a cutting board, sprinkle it with salt and a bit of cumin to taste, cover it loosely with aluminum foil, and allow it to rest for 5 minutes.

7. Meanwhile, strain the pan drippings into the sauce, increase the heat to medium, and bring the sauce to a brief boil again (1 minute). Stir in the cream and chives, simmer gently for 2 minutes, and serve together with the roast.

8. This roast is excellent with salted potatoes, dumplings, or potato croquettes.

Nug Pancakes

Although some see nugs only as pets, they are edible. In fact, nugs constitute a key part of dwarven cuisine, so much so that Varen, the first dwarf to attempt eating a nug—albeit out of desperation—became a paragon for his culinary discovery! I'd liken the flavor to a cross between pork and rabbit. Very tender, especially when roasted. But of all the nug-based dishes I've sampled, my favorite is still the nug pancakes (with nug-gets coming in a close second). I've noted down the recipe here and recommend you give it a try! Of course, if you cannot bring yourself to eat nug, other meats can be substituted in its place.

Yield	*Cook time*	*Difficulty*
3 LARGE SERVINGS	45 MINUTES (PLUS AT LEAST 6 HOURS OF MARINATING AND COOKING)	AVERAGE

Ingredients

"Nug"

2 pounds pork shoulder, one piece, no bones

1 tablespoon salt

1 tablespoon pepper

1½ teaspoons turbinado or raw sugar

1 teaspoon ground coriander

½ teaspoon ground cumin

1 teaspoon hot (spicy Hungarian) paprika

1 teaspoon chili powder

¾ cup plus 1 teaspoon vegetable broth

1 tablespoon olive oil

⅓ cup BBQ sauce (ready-made)

Pancakes

1⅓ cups buttermilk, at room temperature

4 eggs, at room temperature

2½ cups flour

Pinch of salt

2 teaspoons single-acting baking powder

1 tablespoon Italian seasoning

3 tablespoons butter, plus more for frying the pancakes

Equipment

3 long wooden skewers

To make the "nug":

1. Cut the pork shoulder into five equal pieces and transfer to a large freezer bag. Combine the salt, pepper, sugar, coriander, cumin, paprika, and chili powder with the vegetable broth in a bowl. Transfer the marinade to the bag and massage it into the meat on all sides. Then marinate the meat in the refrigerator for at least 3 hours, ideally overnight.

2. Preheat the oven to 325°F.

3. Heat the olive oil in a large oven-safe pot over high heat. Brown the pork shoulder on all sides (about 3 to 4 minutes). Pour in the marinade, cover the pot, set the pot on the center rack of the oven, and cook for 3 hours. Starting halfway through the cooking time, check regularly to make sure there is still enough liquid in the pot. If not, add water. When finished, the liquid should barely cover the base of the pot. The meat is done when it pulls apart effortlessly with a fork. Transfer the meat to a bowl, allow it to cool for 5 minutes, and shred. Add the pan drippings and the barbecue sauce, stir well to combine, and loosely cover the bowl with aluminum foil. Turn off the oven, and keep the bowl warm inside until ready to serve.

To make the pancakes:

4. Using an electric mixer, blend the buttermilk and eggs in a bowl.

5. In a separate bowl, combine the flour, salt, baking powder, and Italian seasoning.

6. Melt the butter in a small pot over medium heat, and add it to the dry ingredients together with the buttermilk mixture. Carefully combine and allow to rest for 15 minutes.

7. Melt a bit of butter (about 1 teaspoon) in a large frying pan over high heat and add 3 to 4 tablespoons of batter per pancake, leaving room between the cakes. Cook each pancake on the first side for 2 to 3 minutes until golden brown; then flip to the other side. Set the pancakes on a plate lined with paper towels and cover loosely with foil. You should have 12 pancakes total.

To assemble:

8. Set one pancake each on three plates and then top with one-ninth of the meat. Set another pancake on top, add more meat, and continue with the next pancake. Repeat with another layer of meat and then a fourth and final pancake. Pierce your creation with a wooden skewer (or a crossbow bolt) and serve immediately.

Fish in Salt Crust

The Avvar are generally rather utilitarian in their cooking methods—lots of stews, which I can hardly find fault with. But holds by lakes and rivers have a unique way of cooking fish. Instead of using a pan, they'll wrap the fish in pungent leaves and salt, then leave it baking all day over banked coals. Like a stew, this method of preparation does not require constant attention. In addition, the salt helps keep moisture inside the fish, which turns the flesh creamy and tender. Plus, there's a great deal of fun to be had when cracking the salt open! It adds a level of drama that I'm sure even the Orlesians would appreciate.

Yield	Cook time	Difficulty
4 SERVINGS	35 MINUTES	AVERAGE

Ingredients

6 egg whites

4½ to 6⅔ pounds salt

2 small whole bass (each about 1⅓ pounds), ready to cook

½ bunch thyme, divided

½ bunch rosemary, divided

1 garlic clove, minced, divided

2 tablespoons olive oil

2 pinches of pepper

2 teaspoons lemon juice

1. In a medium bowl, beat the egg whites with an electric mixer on medium speed until stiff peaks form (about 4 to 5 minutes). Add the salt, and combine thoroughly.

2. Preheat the oven to 400°F. Line a baking sheet with parchment paper.

3. Fill the belly of each fish with a quarter of the thyme, rosemary, and garlic, and brush each fish all over with olive oil.

4. Spread an even layer of salt a little less than ½ inch thick over the baking sheet. Set the fish apart from each other on top of the salt and top each with the remaining thyme, rosemary, and garlic. Spread the rest of the salt mixture evenly over the fish so they are covered on all sides.

5. Bake on the middle rack for about 25 to 35 minutes. To check whether the fish is done, break open the salt crust at the head. If the eyes are white all the way through, the fish is done.

6. To serve, completely break open the salt crust on the top side, and carefully remove it from the fish. Remove the skin, then use two forks to detach the fillets from the bones. Drizzle each fish with 1 teaspoon lemon juice. Enjoy immediately.

Roasted Wyvern

Having made their home in the inhospitable Frostback Mountains, the Avvar live on whatever they can glean from the land, hunting all manner of beasts, from harts and rams to large creatures like lurkers and gurguts—sometimes even wyverns! But take care! Although wyvern can be delicious, if they're not prepared correctly, they're devastatingly poisonous, a consequence of their venomous nature. I've made sure to include detailed instructions. I'm no Antivan Crow like Zevran Arainai, after all; the last thing I want is for anyone to be poisoned via dinner!

Yield	*Cook time*	*Difficulty*
4 SERVINGS	1 HOUR 30 MINUTES (INCLUDING COOKING)	AVERAGE

Ingredients

1 large turkey leg
(about 3⅓ pounds),
ready to cook

2 garlic cloves, minced

3 tablespoons olive oil

2 tablespoons honey

2 tablespoons lemon juice

Salt

Pepper steak seasoning blend

4 sprigs rosemary

1. Preheat the oven to 350°F. Line a baking sheet with parchment paper.

2. Wash the turkey leg and pat dry with paper towels. Pierce the meaty parts of the leg several times with a sharp-pointed knife or kitchen fork.

3. Combine the garlic, olive oil, honey, and lemon juice in a small bowl. Season generously with salt and steak seasoning.

4. Brush the turkey leg on all sides with three-quarters of the garlic oil, and stud the top with the rosemary. Set the leg on the baking sheet, cover loosely with aluminum foil, and cook for 1 hour, brushing it regularly (about every 15 minutes) with more of the garlic oil.

5. Remove the aluminum foil and cook the leg for another 20 minutes, brushing it regularly with the remaining garlic oil mixture. Remove the leg from the oven, and briefly (about 2 to 3 minutes) set it on a plate lined with paper towels to drain. Then set it on a serving plate and enjoy right away.

> This dish pairs excellently with Sera's Yummy Corn (page 103), Honey Carrots (page 107), or Stuffed Deep Mushrooms (page 17).

Nug Bacon and Egg Pie

Ever since I heard about Sister Leliana keeping a nug as a companion, I've desperately longed for a Schmooples of my own. Of course, as adorable as nugs are, allowing them anywhere near a fully stocked kitchen is a recipe for disaster. You'd think that after seeing Mum nearly lose her mind trying to keep the Hero of Ferelden's mabari out of her larder, I'd be a touch more aware of the security of my own roasts. And yet . . . that cute face . . . Suffice it to say, I discovered firsthand just how voracious these little omnivores can be. These days, the closest thing to a nug in my house is this traditional Fereldan farmer's pie.

Contributor	Yield	Cook time	Difficulty
EMILY TAYLOR, SENIOR GAME DESIGNER	1 PIE (ABOUT 6 SERVINGS)	1 HOUR (INCLUDING COOLING AND BAKING)	AVERAGE

Ingredients

Dough
Scant 2 cups flour

1 teaspoon salt

12 tablespoons (1½ sticks) cold butter

Filling
6 to 8 strips nug* bacon

1 small onion, thinly sliced

1 medium tomato, thinly sliced

3 to 4 mushrooms, thinly sliced

6 eggs

2 tablespoons milk

Pinch of salt

Pinch of pepper

2 tablespoons mixed fresh herbs (such as sage, rosemary, and thyme), minced

Equipment
Pie pan (about 9½ inches in diameter)

1 Sift the flour and salt into a bowl. Add the butter, then use two small sharp knives to cut it into pea-size lumps. Add just enough cold water that you can work the ingredients (still using the knife) into a dough firm enough to roll out.

2 Use a rolling pin to roll out the dough as flat as possible on the counter. Then fold the sides in toward the middle, fold again, and refrigerate for 15 minutes.

3 Preheat the oven to 400°F.

4 Divide the dough in half, then roll out each half into a thin circle of dough a little larger than your pie pan. Line the pan with one of the circles. Press it into place on the base and sides. Line evenly with nug bacon. Top with onion, tomato, and mushroom slices.

5 Combine the eggs, milk, salt, pepper, and herbs in a small bowl, and whisk with a fork. Carefully pour the egg mixture into the pie pan. Smooth the top and place the second circle of dough on top. Press together with the bottom piece of dough along the edges to seal the pie, and use a fork to decorate the rim of the pie. Cut away any excess dough with a knife, and cut a couple small slits into the top so that the steam generated during baking can escape.

6 Knead together the dough scraps and decorate the top of the pie with them as desired.

7 Bake for about 30 minutes or until the dough begins to brown.

8 This pie can be enjoyed warm or cold.

*If you can't get nug bacon, any more mundane type of bacon will work.

Starkhaven Fish and Egg Pie

In some ways, this famous pie mirrors its namesake. Not only is it almost oval in shape, but it's also stuffed to the brim with fish from the Minanter River, lending the impression that it, like the city of Starkhaven, sits perched upon the river's bounty. But where the city is crowned with solid rings of tall, gray stone, this pie has a light, flaky crust that, I imagine, is far kinder on one's teeth—not to mention, far tastier! As beautiful as Starkhaven is, with its lavish estates and fountains, I'd much rather take a bite of one of its pies instead. Of course, if Starkhaven's prince were on offer as well . . . just kidding! I'd still take the pie. Given Sebastian Vael's popularity, though, I might be alone in this decision.

Yield	*Cook time*	*Difficulty*
4 TO 5 SERVINGS	1 HOUR 15 MINUTES (INCLUDING BAKING)	AVERAGE

Ingredients

1 cup plus 2 tablespoons white wine

2 onions, diced

2 carrots, diced

1 celery rib, thinly sliced

3 to 4 sprigs dried thyme

2 bay leaves

1 tablespoon sea salt

2 pounds mixed fish (such as carp, trout, or cod), cut into bite-size pieces

9 tablespoons (1 stick plus 1 tablespoon) butter

½ cup flour

17 fluid ounces fish broth

2¼ cups milk

⅔ cup cream

1 tablespoon salt

1 tablespoon pepper

1 tablespoon nutmeg, freshly grated

1.75 ounces dried currants

3 eggs, hard-boiled and sliced

9 ounces pie dough, store-bought

1 egg, beaten

Head and tail of any fish desired, for garnishing

Fresh mint leaves, for garnishing

1.75 ounces almonds, peeled, for garnishing

Equipment
Casserole dish (8½ by 11 inches)

1   Fill as large a pot as possible with 3 quarts of water. Add the wine, onions, carrots, celery, thyme, bay leaves, and sea salt. Heat over medium heat until the mixture steams, then carefully add the fish, making sure the fish is completely covered by the liquid. Simmer, stirring occasionally, for 15 minutes. When the fish is done, use a skimmer to remove it and set aside.

2   Melt the butter in a separate small pot over medium heat. Add the flour and stir for 2 minutes. Gradually pour in the fish broth and milk, working with a little less than ½ cup at a time, and whisk vigorously after each addition until all of the liquid has been absorbed. Bring to a boil and simmer, stirring frequently, for at least 10 minutes. If the sauce seems too thick, add a bit of broth or milk as needed.

3   Remove from heat and stir in the cream. Season generously with salt, pepper, and nutmeg. Fold in the fish, currants, and eggs, then spoon the mixture into the casserole dish, spreading it in an even layer.

4   Preheat the oven to 350°F.

5   Use a rolling pin to roll out the pie dough until you have a round a little larger than your casserole dish. Brush the edges of the dish with the beaten egg. Lay the dough over the top of the dish, leaving a little overhang, and use a small sharp knife to cut a slit in the dough at the front and back so you can insert the fish head and tail under the dough there. Press the dough lightly into place over the fish parts. Arrange the mint leaves between the head and tail so they are reminiscent of bones (see picture). Space out the almonds along the edges of the casserole dish.

6   Use your fingertips to press the dough against the rim of the casserole dish, then cut away all excess dough. Brush the top of the pie with the remaining egg and make a few small cuts in the dough so the moisture generated during baking can escape. Bake for 30 minutes until the crust is golden brown and the filling is bubbling. Remove the pie from the oven, allow it to stand for 2 minutes, and then serve promptly in the casserole dish.

The fish head and tail pictured are purely decorative and don't necessarily need to be eaten.

Cacio e Pepe

A classic Antivan dish that graces the tables of both rich and poor alike. Composed of three main ingredients—pasta, cheese, and pepper—cacio e pepe is delightfully simple. And yet, it is also very easy to get wrong, as I quickly discovered. The sauce must be smooth, not clumpy, a surprisingly tall ask when your tools are dry cheese and water. But do not despair! This skill, like all others, can be learned, and with a bit of practice, you too will be able to make a sauce that even the most scrutinizing of Antivan grandmothers can't help but approve of. And let me tell you, that nod of approval is worth every ounce of struggle. So let me be the first to offer it to you, as Mum did for me when I was a child helping her in the kitchen: I'm so proud of you for persevering!

Yield	Cook time	Difficulty
4 SERVINGS	20 MINUTES	EASY

Ingredients

Pinch of salt, plus more for the pasta water

14 ounces spaghetti or linguine, preferably fresh

1 tablespoon mixed black peppercorns

1 teaspoon vegetable oil

1 red onion, diced

7 ounces Pecorino Romano cheese, freshly grated, plus more for garnishing

Bit of red pepperweed (pepper grass), for garnishing

Equipment

Mortar and pestle

1   Generously salt a large pot of water, and bring to a boil over medium heat. When the water boils, add the pasta; cook, stirring occasionally, until it is al dente. How long this takes depends on the type of pasta used: Consult the package and subtract 2 minutes from that recommended cook time.

2   Transfer the peppercorns to a mortar and carefully crush with the pestle. Then transfer the crushed pepper to a large frying pan and toast it over low heat without adding any fat or oil (about 2 to 3 minutes). Remove the pepper, add the vegetable oil, and heat through. Add the onions to the pan and sweat briefly (1 to 2 minutes). Add the pepper back in. Use a ladle to remove ½ ladleful pasta water from the pasta pot and use it to deglaze the frying pan.

3   When the pasta is cooked, strain it, reserving 4 to 5 ladles of the pasta water. Allow the pasta to drain, then transfer a third of it to the frying pan with the pepper. Using a pair of pasta tongs, carefully combine. If the dish seems too dry, add a bit of pasta water.

4   Transfer half of the grated cheese to a bowl. Add a ladle of pasta water, and whisk briskly. Then add the remaining cheese and more pasta water, and whisk until you have a nice, creamy cheese sauce.

5   Add the remaining pasta to the pan, and turn off the heat. Pour the creamy cheese sauce over the pasta, season to taste with a pinch of salt, and combine thoroughly. Arrange on deep plates, and sprinkle with more grated cheese to serve. Garnish to taste with a bit of fresh pepperweed.

You can also use freshly ground black pepper instead of pepperweed to prepare this dish.

Turnip and Mutton Pie

I already know what you're thinking. A Fereldan about to extol the virtues of turnips? Of course! They're a wonderful little root vegetable, capable of being prepared any number of ways—whether boiled, stir-fried, roasted, steamed, or mashed—and even eaten raw! Although they certainly make a great addition to any stew, for now, I'd like to introduce you to the wonders of turnips in pies.

This particular pie is a classic Fereldan dish served at taverns across the kingdom. Tender chunks of lamb and turnip are enveloped in a buttery crust that, together, never fail to put a smile on my face. It doesn't matter how cold or miserable the day is. None of that is any match for a belly full of warm, rich, turnipy goodness. Even just the smell alone is a comfort that no other food could ever hope to match. And although you could certainly evoke it by throwing a bushel of turnips into the fire, as Cole once did, I think putting them in a pie is a much tastier idea.

Yield	Cook time	Difficulty
4 TO 5 SERVINGS	2 HOURS 20 MINUTES (INCLUDING COOKING AND BAKING)	AVERAGE

Ingredients

2¼ pounds lamb neck fillet, cut into bite-size pieces

2 tablespoons flour

3 tablespoons vegetable oil

2 onions, diced

1 teaspoon salt, plus more as needed

1 teaspoon pepper, plus more as needed

2 sprigs rosemary

3½ cups chicken or poultry stock

14 ounces rutabagas, cut into bite-size pieces

5.3 ounces dried fruit (such as apricots, cranberries, or prunes), coarsely chopped

¼ bunch parsley, freshly chopped

9 ounces frozen puff pastry sheets (store-bought), thawed

1 egg, beaten

Equipment

Pie pan (about 11 inches in diameter)

1   Put the lamb in a bowl and generously sprinkle with flour.

2   In a heavy-bottomed pot, heat the vegetable oil over medium heat. Add the onion and sweat until translucent (1 to 2 minutes). Then add the lamb and brown on all sides (about 3 to 4 minutes). Season with salt and pepper. Add the rosemary and pour in the stock. Simmer, stirring occasionally, for 90 minutes or until the meat is tender and the sauce has thickened considerably. Regularly skim off the fat that collects on the surface (about every 10 minutes).

3   When the time is up, add the rutabaga and dried fruit, cover, and add water as needed to fully cover the rutabaga. Simmer for about 15 minutes. Then remove the pot from heat, stir in the parsley, and season to taste with salt and pepper.

4   Preheat the oven to 400°F.

5   Use a rolling pin to roll out the pastry a little less than ¼ inch thick. Then use a small sharp knife to cut the pastry so that it will fit your pie pan with about ¾ inch of overhang on all sides.

6   Fill the pie pan with the meat-and-rutabaga mixture, and smooth the top. Brush the edges of the dough with the egg, and set the dough, egg side down, on top of the pan. Use a fork to press the dough into place along the edges. Use a small sharp knife to cut a slit about ¾ inch to a little less than 1¼ inches in the top of the pie so that the steam generated during baking can escape. Then brush the pie with the remaining egg, and bake in the preheated oven for about 20 minutes.

7   This pie is excellent paired with salted or mashed potatoes.

Smoked Ham from the Anderfels

Contrary to what the rumors (or perhaps just the importers) would have you believe, this ham does not taste of despair—whatever flavor that might be. Although the Anderfels are largely ill-suited to farming, pigs do surprisingly well there, in spite of the notoriously inhospitable climate. As a result, ham from the Anderfels is generous in size and, when glazed, makes for a delicious meal. In terms of glazes, my personal favorite is made from a combination of apples and apricots. However, I've heard that one glaze, in particular, made from wildflowers, can turn a smoked ham as hard as jade! Not at all suitable for eating, but I imagine it would pack quite the punch, especially in the hands of a warrior like Divine Victoria!

Yield	Cook time	Difficulty
5 TO 6 SERVINGS	1 HOUR 30 MINUTES	AVERAGE

Ingredients

2 tablespoons clarified butter (ghee)

1 onion, diced

2 tablespoons apple cider vinegar

⅔ cup chicken or poultry stock

3 tablespoons apricot jam

1 tablespoon honey

1 teaspoon pepper

1 whole smoked ham (about 3⅓ pounds)

Equipment

Casserole dish (about 8½ by 11 inches)

1 Heat the ghee in a small pot over medium heat. Add the onion and sweat until translucent (about 2 minutes). Add the vinegar, stock, jam, honey, and pepper and reduce significantly, stirring frequently, for 15 minutes. Remove from heat.

2 Meanwhile, preheat the oven to 350°F.

3 Brush the ham on all sides with the glaze, and set it in the casserole dish. Pour the rest of the glaze over it, and then set the casserole dish on the center rack of the oven. Bake for 60 minutes, turning the ham over regularly every 10 minutes and brushing it with the glaze that collects in the pan.

4 When the cooking time is done, remove the pan from the oven and allow the ham to rest in the pan for 5 minutes before serving.

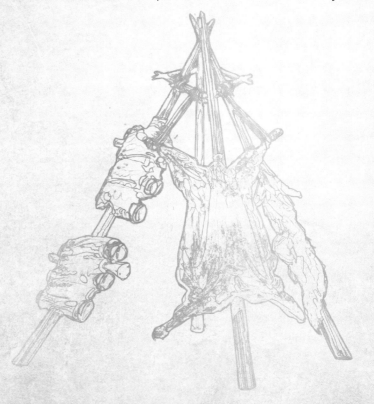

Roasted Turkey with Sides

If you're attending the Prince of Starkhaven's birthday celebration or any dinner party in the Free Marches, chances are, you'll find this feast waiting for you. The roasted turkey, cooked to golden-brown perfection, sits surrounded by a host of different sides, creating a picturesque scene that's certain to impress everyone lucky enough to secure an invite.

Unsurprisingly, this culinary tableau is far from a quick-and-easy meal. The chef who prepared the rendition I enjoyed in Kirkwall informed me—after much persuasion—that the turkey alone took hours to prepare. Add a few sides, and there goes most of the day, especially if you don't have a full set of kitchen staff to assist you! Unfortunately, I discovered this the hard way when I later attempted to put this recipe into practice. By the time everything was properly cooked and ready, it was late into the evening—well past dinnertime, even in Antiva, where dinner is usually a late-night affair. So take my advice, and budget more time than you think you need. Also be sure to invite some friends! This is definitely a meal that's meant to be shared, which, in my opinion, makes it the best kind!

Yield	Cook time	Difficulty
6 SERVINGS	5 TO 6 HOURS (INCLUDING COOKING)	AVERAGE

Ingredients

Turkey

2 onions, diced

1 apple (tart), cored, peeled, and diced

3.5 ounces chicken or turkey liver, diced

9 ounces ground pork

½ celery rib, minced

1 garlic clove, minced

½ bunch fresh parsley, minced

⅔ cup chicken broth

Freshly ground black pepper

3 tablespoons olive oil

3 tablespoons paprika

1 teaspoon salt

1 turkey (about 9 pounds), ready to cook

Sauce

2 tablespoons orange juice

3 tablespoons plus 1 teaspoon white wine

2 tablespoons cranberry sauce (or preserves)

3 tablespoons plus 1 teaspoon cream

Brown gravy thickener (optional)

To make the turkey:

1   Combine the onions, apple, liver, pork, celery, garlic, and parsley in a bowl with the broth. Season with a bit of freshly ground black pepper.

2   Preheat the oven to 350°F. Set a large bowl or roasting pan with an inch of water inside on the bottom of the oven to catch the drippings.

3   Combine the olive oil, paprika, salt, and a generous pinch of black pepper in a small bowl.

4   Thoroughly rinse the turkey, pat dry with paper towels, and fill with the ground meat mixture. Close the "opening" with toothpicks, set the turkey on a roasting rack, and brush the turkey all over with the seasoned marinade. Then set the turkey on the lowest rack of the oven, and cook for about 4 to 5 hours, depending on the weight. The rule of thumb here is 1 hour of cooking time for every 2¼ pounds of meat. Generously brush with the drippings from the bowl or pan at regular intervals (every 15 minutes), and turn over once an hour. During this time, prepare the side dishes.

5   When the turkey is done, turn off the oven, and loosely cover the turkey with aluminum foil to keep it warm.

6   Set the turkey on a cutting board to serve, and carve as desired with a pair of shears. Remove the stuffing. Serve the turkey with the filling, sauce, and sides.

To make the sauce:

7   Strain the drippings from the bowl or roasting pan into a small pot, and combine with the orange juice, white wine, and cranberry sauce. Bring to a boil over medium heat, and then immediately reduce the heat to low and stir in the cream. If the sauce is too thin, thicken it with a bit of gravy thickener. Keep warm until ready to serve.

Continued on page 98

Potato Wedges

1¾ pounds potatoes
(firm, waxy variety)

4 tablespoons oil

2 garlic cloves, minced

1½ teaspoons salt

1½ teaspoons pepper

1½ teaspoons paprika

Brussels Sprouts

1¾ pounds Brussels sprouts

¼ cup (½ stick) butter

Pinch of salt

Pinch of pepper

Generous pinch of nutmeg, grated

Red Cabbage

1 head red cabbage
(about 2¼ pounds)

¼ cup plus 2 teaspoons
clarified butter (ghee)

1 onion, diced

1 apple (tart), peeled,
cored, and diced

2 tablespoons sugar,
plus more as needed

2 tablespoons apple cider
vinegar, plus more as needed

2 bay leaves

5 whole cloves

5 juniper berries

1 tablespoon bouillon powder

Pinch of salt,
plus more as needed

4 teaspoons brandy

Equipment

Toothpicks

To make the potato wedges:

8 Preheat the oven to 350°F. Line a baking sheet with parchment paper.

9 Thoroughly wash the potatoes, dry them, and cut them into quarters, leaving the peel on.

10 Combine the oil, garlic, salt, pepper, and paprika in a large bowl. Add the potato wedges and combine thoroughly so the potatoes are coated with seasoning on all sides. Spread on the baking sheet so the wedges do not overlap and bake for 40 to 50 minutes until the potatoes are golden brown or as crisp as desired, turning occasionally.

11 Keep warm in the oven until ready to serve.

To make the Brussels sprouts:

12 Wash and dry the Brussels sprouts. Use a small sharp knife to remove the outer, spotty leaves from each sprout. Then trim each stem a bit and make a crosswise cut in it (about ¼ inch deep) so the sprout will cook as evenly as possible.

13 Bring a medium pot of water to a boil over medium heat. Add the Brussels sprouts and cook for about 15 minutes or until they are tender and cooked through. Transfer to a strainer and drain thoroughly.

14 Meanwhile, melt the butter in a large frying pan over medium heat. Add the Brussels sprouts and brown on all sides for 2 to 3 minutes, swirling the pan regularly. Finally, season with salt, pepper, and nutmeg. Keep warm on the stove until ready to serve.

To make the red cabbage:

15 Wash the cabbage and pat dry. Remove the outer leaves and quarter the cabbage with a large serrated knife. Then use a small sharp knife, such as a paring knife, to cut the stalk part out of each quarter in a wedge shape. Slice the cabbage quarters into strips about ⅛ inch to just less than ¼ inch wide.

16 Melt the ghee in a large pot over medium heat. Add the onion and sweat for 2 to 3 minutes until translucent. Add the apple and sugar and cook for 1 to 2 minutes. Then add the red cabbage, apple cider vinegar, bay leaves, cloves, juniper berries, bouillon powder, salt, and brandy to the pot. Stir well to combine. Cover and cook, stirring occasionally, for about 45 minutes or until the cabbage is cooked and tender.

17 Remove the cloves and juniper berries, and dispose of them. Season to taste with more salt, vinegar, or sugar. Keep warm on the stove until ready to serve.

Sides

Sera's Yummy Corn

This recipe is simple, yet strict. No wraps. No non-yellow corn. Peel halfway, then wash and cook; peel again, and eat.

    Personally, I think other varieties of corn would work just fine—I agree with checking for rot, of course—but the suggestion was met with such disgust from Sera that, well, I couldn't bring myself to try it. Also, while the original recipe advises acquiring the ingredients through less-than-honorable means, let me assure you that merchant-bought corn is absolutely fine. Friends of Red Jenny can, of course, pilfer a few ears from an undeserving noble, as usual.

Yield	Cook time	Difficulty
4 SERVINGS	25 MINUTES	AVERAGE

Ingredients

Herb Butter
1 bunch curly parsley, minced

½ bunch chives, minced

1 garlic clove, minced

1 red onion, diced

10½ tablespoons salted butter, softened

1 teaspoon ground mustard

1 teaspoon chili flakes

Corn on the Cob
4 cobs sweet corn (precooked)

⅓ cup plus 2 tablespoons milk

1 tablespoon sugar

1 red chili pepper, sliced into thin rings, for garnishing

To make the herb butter:

1 Combine the parsley, chives, garlic, onion, butter, ground mustard, and chili flakes in a small bowl and knead thoroughly with a fork. Wrap in waxed paper and shape into a log, or refrigerate right in the bowl until used.

To make the corn:

2 Place the whole corn in a medium pot and add just enough water to cover. Add the milk and sugar and bring to a boil over medium heat. Cover and cook for about 7 to 9 minutes.

3 Turn on your oven's grill or broiler function. Line a baking sheet with parchment paper.

4 Take the cooked corn out of the water, and drain thoroughly. Brush each cob with herb butter on all sides, and set it on the baking sheet. If you're using the grill function at the top of the oven, place the baking sheet in the top position and grill the corn for 5 to 6 minutes, turning it regularly and brushing melted herb butter from the pan back over the corn with each turning. Follow the same process if you're using the broiler.

5 Remove the cooked corn from the oven. Brush generously with herb butter again, sprinkle with chili rings to taste, and serve with the rest of the herb butter.

Stuffed Vine Leaves

The first thing I did upon arriving in the Tevinter Imperium was head for the nearest tavern and order this classic Tevinter appetizer. These tender leaves are stuffed with rice, herbs, and sometimes minced meat. When topped with a bit of lemon juice and a dollop of tzatziki sauce, they're sure to leave you in a state of bliss with just a single bite. In my case, I was so enchanted by the delicious flavors that I didn't even notice the commotion outside! Apparently, there was a disagreement between a magister and another magister's son—about what, I couldn't say. After all, I was too busy eating!

Yield	Cook time	Difficulty
4 SERVINGS	1 HOUR 30 MINUTES (PLUS 12 HOURS FOR COOLING)	AVERAGE

Ingredients

10 tablespoons olive oil, divided

2 onions, diced

¾ cup rice

Pinch of salt

1 tablespoon raisins

Pinch of dried mint

Pinch of dried dill

Pinch of dried fennel

8.8 ounces fresh grape leaves

Juice of 1 lemon

1. Heat 2 tablespoons olive oil in a medium pot over medium heat. Add the onion and sweat until translucent on all sides (about 2 to 3 minutes). Add the rice and cover completely with water; stir in the salt. Cover and simmer for about 20 minutes or until the rice has absorbed nearly all the liquid.

2. Remove the rice from the heat, and stir in the raisins, mint, dill, and fennel. Set aside.

3. Transfer the leaves to a bowl, and cover with boiling water. Soak for about 3 to 5 minutes. Then carefully put the leaves in a pasta strainer (so they do not tear), and rinse briefly with cold water.

4. To fill the leaves, set each one on the counter, ribbed side up, and put 1 tablespoon of herbed rice in the middle. Now fold in the sides of the leaf, roll the leaf together firmly, and shape it into a little sausage shape. Set the rolled vine leaves in a large pot.

5. Combine the remaining olive oil with the lemon juice and 2¼ cups water. Pour the mixture over the stuffed leaves in the pot, cover, and bring to a simmer over low heat. Simmer for about 45 minutes or until the stuffed leaves have soaked up all the liquid.

6. Set the stuffed leaves on a large plate, cover loosely with plastic wrap, and refrigerate overnight so the flavors can meld.

7. This dish is excellent served with Nevarran Flat Bread and the accompanying creamy, savory yogurt dip (page 109).

Honey Carrots

In much the same way as the Inquisition is to the Inquisitor, a meal is more than just the main course. Sides form an equal part of the equation and deserve just as much care and attention as the dish they're served alongside. It's a lesson Mum taught me long ago and one I haven't forgotten since. So of course, I noticed when this Orlesian staple made an appearance. It graced my table not once, not twice, but every single time I dined in Orlais. And while I enjoyed the traditional Orlesian rendition of this dish—which is on the sweeter side, thanks to a liberal application of honey—those who prefer a level of sweetness more in line with a carrot's natural flavor should employ a lighter touch.

Yield	Cook time	Difficulty
4 SERVINGS	20 MINUTES	AVERAGE

Ingredients

2¼ pounds baby carrots

2 tablespoons olive oil

Salt

Freshly ground black pepper

Scant ½ cup vegetable broth

Juice of 1 lemon

2 tablespoons honey

1 tablespoon balsamic vinegar

3 to 4 sprigs thyme,
with the leaves plucked off

1 Wash, clean, and peel the carrots whole, leaving some of the green part intact.

2 Transfer the olive oil to as large a frying pan as possible, and heat over medium heat. When the oil is hot, add the carrots, lined up next to each other, and brown on all sides (about 3 to 4 minutes). Season to taste with salt and pepper, deglaze with the broth, and stir in the lemon juice. Cover and cook the carrots until they are firm to the bite (about 5 to 7 minutes).

3 Remove the lid when the cooking time is over. Drizzle the carrots evenly with the honey and balsamic vinegar, and cook for another 4 to 5 minutes until done. While the carrots are cooking, brush them repeatedly with the honey sauce from the pan.

4 Set the carrots on a serving plate, and pour the reduced sauce from the pan over them. Sprinkle with the thyme leaves. Season to taste with salt, pepper, and lemon juice.

5 These carrots are perfect served as a side with hearty main dishes such as Roasted Turkey with Sides (page 97) or Gurgut Roast with Lowlander Spices and Mushroom Sauce (page 79).

Nevarran Flat Bread and Yogurt Dip

There's something supremely satisfying about a tall stack of Nevarran flat bread—and I don't just mean in the aesthetic sense. Of course, being pleasing to the eye is certainly a consideration. This is a Nevarran dish, after all. But the process of being able to go from dough to ready-to-eat bread in minutes reaches a whole level of satisfaction on its own, especially if you're used to waiting hours for a loaf to finish baking! Best of all, this bread can be eaten in a variety of different ways, whether on its own, brushed with oil, or as a vehicle for an assortment of dips. Personally, I'd love to try it with a good stew from home one day.

Yield	Cook time	Difficulty
4 SERVINGS	6 HOURS 40 MINUTES (INCLUDING STANDING AND BAKING)	AVERAGE

Ingredients

Yogurt Dip
1 cucumber

2 tablespoons salt, plus more to taste

1 small carrot, finely grated

4 garlic cloves, minced

18 ounces Greek yogurt

2 tablespoons olive oil

1 tablespoon lemon juice

Pepper

2 sprigs fresh mint, leaves only, minced

Flat Bread
4 cups plus 2 tablespoons wheat flour, plus more for the counter

5½ tablespoons salt

2 teaspoons olive oil, plus more for the bowl

2 teaspoons sugar

1 package active dry yeast

1½ cups plus 4 teaspoons water

1 egg

Black cumin seed, for sprinkling

Equipment
Grater

To make the yogurt dip:

1. Wash and peel the cucumber, then cut it in half lengthwise. Use a small sharp knife to cut out the core. Grate the cucumber and transfer it to a bowl. Stir in the salt and allow to stand for 30 minutes. Then strain, collecting the cucumber water below the strainer.

2. Transfer the grated cucumber to a clean dish towel and use your hands to squeeze out as much of the remaining liquid as possible into a small bowl.

3. Combine the carrot, garlic, yogurt, cucumber liquid, and cucumber in a large bowl. Stir well to combine. Season with olive oil and lemon juice, and then generously season to taste with salt and pepper. Cover loosely with plastic wrap and refrigerate for at least 6 hours (ideally overnight) for the flavors to meld.

4. Before serving, stir thoroughly and fold in a bit of freshly chopped mint. The dip is best enjoyed slightly chilled.

To make the flat bread:

5. Combine the flour, salt, oil, sugar, yeast, and water in a bowl, and knead by hand until a very soft dough forms (about 8 minutes). Transfer to a separate oiled bowl. Cover the bowl with a clean dish towel and allow the dough to stand in a warm place for 90 minutes.

6. Transfer the dough to a lightly floured surface, and divide it into four equal portions. Shape the pieces of dough by hand into a somewhat oval form, and press lightly to flatten. Set the dough on a baking sheet lined with parchment paper. Cover the baking sheet with a clean dish towel, and allow the dough to stand for 20 minutes.

7. Whisk the egg and 1 teaspoon water in a cup. Brush the tops of the dough with the egg wash, then sprinkle with black cumin seed to taste. Allow the dough to stand, covered, for another 20 minutes.

8. Preheat the oven to 475°F.

9. Bake the flat bread for about 7 to 9 minutes until golden brown; then remove it from the oven and allow it to cool on the baking sheet for 5 minutes. Serve as promptly as possible with the yogurt dip. The bread is also excellent with Stuffed Vine Leaves (page 105).

Sweet Delights

Blancmange

When translated literally from Orlesian, blancmange means "white eating," which, I suppose, is pretty accurate. This dish is a white pudding made with either milk or heavy cream that's been thickened. On its own, it possesses a relatively mild sweetness—particularly by Orlesian standards. But that's because it's generally served with various toppings, such as a red grape compote, to amplify the dish's sweet flavors. The toppings are also a great way to decorate an otherwise plain-looking dessert. I've seen everything from designs composed of toasted almonds to ribbons of fresh mango. There's really no limit to what you can do!

If you're looking for a particularly elegant option, you need only turn to Lady Vivienne for guidance. After all, she's the veritable queen of style, no matter the medium. When it comes to the blancmange, her preferred arrangement remains true to the dish's name, offering a pristine white-on-white tableau of white chocolate curls and whole jasmine flowers. The result is gorgeous on its own, but when served on a dark plate, it looks all the more stunning!

As stunning as that is, I prefer to add a cherry sauce to top the dish.

Yield	Cook time	Difficulty
4 SERVINGS	5 HOURS 45 MINUTES (INCLUDING COOLING)	AVERAGE

Ingredients

Blancmange
5 sheets white gelatin

1 cup plus 2 tablespoons milk

3.5 ounces ground almonds, without skins

¼ cup sugar

½ vanilla bean

1 cup plus 2 tablespoons heavy whipping cream

2 to 3 drops almond extract

Cherry Sauce
14 ounces sour cherries, from a jar or can, with juice

1 tablespoon lemon juice

1 tablespoon cornstarch

3 tablespoons sugar

Pinch of cinnamon

Equipment
4 dessert molds or ramekins (each with a capacity of about 5 ounces)

1 Soak the gelatin in a small bowl of cold water, according to the package directions.

2 Combine the milk, almonds, sugar, and the vanilla bean in a medium pot over medium heat and bring to a boil, stirring frequently. Remove from heat and allow to stand, covered, for 20 minutes for the flavors to meld. Strain into a medium bowl. Add the cream and almond extract and stir well to combine.

3 Gently squeeze the gelatin to remove excess fluid, and then add it to the vanilla almond milk. Stir until the gelatin has dissolved completely.

4 Rinse out the dessert molds with cold water and fill evenly with the almond mixture. Smooth the tops. If the molds do not have lids of their own, cover them with plastic wrap. Refrigerate for at least 5 hours (ideally overnight).

5 Meanwhile, prepare the cherry sauce. Pour the cherries and cherry juice into a small pot. Add the lemon juice, starch, sugar, and cinnamon and bring to a boil over medium heat. Reduce the heat to low and simmer for about 10 to 15 minutes or until the mixture has thickened noticeably, stirring as little as possible in the process so the cherries do not fall apart. Remove from heat, and allow to cool briefly before serving.

6 When the blancmange has cooled, carefully transfer each serving onto a small plate, and garnish to taste with cherry sauce. Serve immediately.

Poison Stings

Traveling is exhausting, as I've recently discovered. Even if you're just sitting in a carriage, it can often feel like you're walking every step of the way. Thankfully, I'm not the first to take long journeys across Thedas. Dorian Pavus traveled all the way from Tevinter to Ferelden in order to join the Inquisition—and rather quickly, at that! His secret? Chocolate-coated orange peels, colloquially known as poison stings. They're sweet and sour, crunchy and chewy, and certain to perk you right up whenever you're starting to feel a bit worn down.

Yield	Cook time	Difficulty
ABOUT 20 PIECES	30 MINUTES	AVERAGE

Ingredients

2 large organic oranges

5 tablespoons sugar

2 tablespoons water

½ cup plus 4 teaspoons milk chocolate

1   Carefully wash and dry the oranges. Use a small sharp kitchen knife to slice them from top to bottom, spacing the cuts a little over 1 inch apart. Carefully remove the peel from the fruit, and cut it in a "sting" shape (see the accompanying picture).

2   Line a baking sheet with parchment paper.

3   Transfer the sugar and water to a nonstick frying pan, and heat over medium heat, stirring frequently, until white bubbles form (about 3 to 5 minutes). Lay the orange strips in the pan and caramelize on both sides for about 1 to 2 minutes each, making sure the orange peel does not get too dark in the process (otherwise, it will taste too bitter). Carefully remove the finished strips from the pan, set them on the baking sheet, and allow them to cool for 5 minutes.

4   Meanwhile, melt the chocolate in a double boiler or bain-marie or by heating in 10-second intervals in the microwave.

5   Dip one end of each cooled orange strip about one-third deep into the melted chocolate. Return it to the baking sheet and allow the chocolate to dry for several minutes before consuming.

Dalish Forest Fruit Cobbler

Mum always knew there's no greater comfort than a warm slice of cobbler—and the Dalish know it, too! The first time I had a bite of this dessert, it was like sitting in Mum's kitchen all over again, letting the simple pleasure of her baking wash away the day's troubles. Hard to feel the sting of a skinned knee or a lost game when your belly is full of warm, gooey goodness, no? Although Mum usually made her cobblers with strawberries and rhubarb—only the stems, of course, as the leaves are poisonous—you can follow the Dalish's lead and use whatever forest fruit is currently in season.

Contributor	Yield	Cook time	Difficulty
EMILY TAYLOR, SENIOR GAME DESIGNER	5 TO 6 SERVINGS	75 MINUTES (INCLUDING STANDING AND BAKING)	AVERAGE

Ingredients

18 ounces fresh fruit (such as strawberries, blueberries, or cherries), plus more for garnishing

1 cup sugar (less if the fruit is very sweet), divided

9 tablespoons (1 stick plus 1 tablespoon) salted butter

1⅔ cups flour

3 teaspoons single-acting baking powder

½ teaspoon salt

¾ cup buttermilk

2 teaspoons turbinado or raw sugar

Ice cream

Equipment

Casserole dish (about 5 by 10 inches)

1   Wash the fruit and cut it into bite-size pieces as needed. Transfer the fruit to a bowl and sprinkle with ⅔ cup of the sugar. Stir well to combine, and allow to stand for 30 minutes. Pour off any excess liquid, add the rest of the sugar, and stir well to combine.

2   Heat the butter in the microwave until it is very soft, and then transfer it to a separate bowl. Stir in the flour, baking powder, and salt, and combine until the mixture resembles coarse breading. Then add the buttermilk and stir with a spoon until a thick, sticky dough forms.

3   Preheat the oven to 425°F.

4   Arrange the fruit in an even layer in the casserole dish. Then top with an even layer of streusel dough and sprinkle with the turbinado or raw sugar.

5   Bake for about 25 to 30 minutes or until the top has begun to brown. Remove from the oven and allow to cool for 5 minutes. Serve garnished with ice cream and fresh fruit, to taste.

Dwarven Plum Jam

One of the great joys of this journey has been the sheer variety of foods I've encountered. However, there are certain places that, by nature of their climate or simply location, offer little in the way of choice when it comes to locally produced foods. The dwarven city of Orzammar is one such place.

Though it is underground, the city is by no means isolated, and trade with the surface has ensured that foods from above ground have soared to great heights of popularity below. Jam, particularly that made from plums, seems to be in especially high demand. The price, however, was enough to make my eyes water! It's no surprise that only the wealthiest and most influential residents of Orzammar can afford it.

That's not to say that the rest of the city's population is doomed to live a jamless existence! While in Orzammar, I spoke to a local jam maker who, rather than purchase the jams directly from merchants, has opted to import only the individual components. They hope that, by making the actual preserves themselves, they can sell their product for a much more reasonable price. And the results, I dare say, were very sweet.

Yield	Cook time	Difficulty
4 TO 5 JARS OF JAM	40 MINUTES	AVERAGE

Ingredients

2½ pounds plums

Juice of 1 large lemon

5 teaspoons agar-agar

1 tablespoon ground cinnamon

1 tablespoon vanilla extract

Equipment

Immersion blender

4 to 5 boiled preserving jars (each large enough to hold about 14 ounces)

1. Wash and dry the plums, remove the pits with a small sharp knife, and weigh the fruit until you have 2½ pounds. When you have the right amount, cut the plums into small pieces (about 1 to 2 inches) and transfer the fruit to a large pot.

2. Pour lemon juice evenly over the plums and heat over medium heat. Reduce the heat to low. Stirring constantly, simmer for about 5 to 8 minutes or until the plums are soft enough to purée with the immersion blender.

3. Purée the plums very coarsely. Stir in the agar-agar, cinnamon, and vanilla extract. Increase the heat to medium and bring to a boil. Boil, stirring frequently, for about 5 to 6 minutes or until the mixture jells. Divide the jam between the prepared preserving jars. Close the jars and allow to cool completely. Store the jars in the refrigerator.

4. The plum jam will keep for up to 6 months sealed in a cool place. Refrigerate after opening.

Sour Cherries in Cream

Imagine that you, like me, are at a dinner party in Orlais. You've just finished polishing off the second-to-last course, the latest in a long slew of extravagance, and you're starting to realize that perhaps you overindulged earlier in the evening. But how could you not? The food was just so good. Now there's only dessert left, and your stomach feels like it's about to burst. At this point, you cannot imagine how you'll manage to choke down whatever tower of sugar and cream awaits you in the kitchens. All you know is that you have to. You cannot be rude to your host, after all. What a relief, then, when dessert finally arrives, and you're presented with a small bowl filled with black cherries dressed in sweet cherry sauce and whipped cream. Evidently, even the Orlesians are sometimes in need of lighter fare. And so the night ends, with stomachs still intact and no offense caused. A happy ending for all!

Yield	Cook time	Difficulty
4 SERVINGS	20 MINUTES	AVERAGE

Ingredients

¼ cup sugar

¾ cup plus 2 tablespoons red wine

¾ cup plus 2 tablespoons cherry juice (from the cherries)

½ cinnamon stick

½ vanilla bean, cut open lengthwise

12 teaspoons cherry liqueur

1 teaspoon cornstarch

14 ounces sour cherries (from a jar), drained

⅔ cup whipping cream

8 scoops ice cream, any flavor

1 Transfer the sugar to a medium pot and heat over high heat until it is golden brown and begins to bubble slightly. Then deglaze with the red wine and cherry juice.

2 Lower the heat to medium. Add the cinnamon stick and vanilla bean and simmer, stirring occasionally, for 10 minutes.

3 Meanwhile, combine 8 teaspoons of cherry liqueur and the cornstarch in a cup.

4 Remove the cinnamon and vanilla from the pot. Add the cherries, stir in the cherry liqueur mixture, and bring to a brief boil (about 2 to 3 minutes). Remove from heat.

5 Combine the cream and remaining cherry liqueur in a mixing cup or bowl and beat with an electric mixer until creamy (about 3 to 4 minutes).

6 Divide the cream among four dessert bowls. Add two scoops of ice cream to each, garnish with cherries to taste, and drizzle with cherry sauce.

7 Serve immediately.

Treviso Energy Balls

As a Fereldan, I'm no stranger to hardship. The Fifth Blight took much from us, but the darkspawn are hardly the sole cause of suffering in Thedas. Take Treviso, a port city in northern Antiva, for example: Treviso was captured and liberated several times during both the Qunari Wars and the New Exalted Marches. As you can imagine, during times of occupation, food was scarce, and those living in the city had to make do with the limited ingredients they still had. Of course, people can be remarkably creative, particularly in difficult times. You need only look to the work Anders did in his clinic in Darktown to know that much. And so the Treviso energy ball was born, combining peanut butter, oats, and dried fruits into a bite-size treat that's just bursting with energy! Perfect for when you're out sabotaging weapon caches—or just taking a hike.

Contributor	Yield	Cook time	Difficulty
HAREL EILAM, GAME ECONOMY DESIGNER	24 ENERGY BALLS	45 MINUTES (INCLUDING COOLING)	AVERAGE

Ingredients

21 ounces dried dates

7 ounces raisins

3.5 ounces peanut butter

⅔ cup instant oats

1 cup plus 2 tablespoons rolled oats

1   Place the dates and raisins in a bowl large enough to hold them, and cover completely with boiling water. Soak for 5 minutes, then strain and allow to drain thoroughly.

2   Add the fruit to the bowl of a stand mixer or food processor and process to a fine paste. Add the peanut butter and instant oats and mix until a uniform mass forms.

3   Transfer the rolled oats to a bowl.

4   With slightly moistened hands, shape the fruit-and-peanut-butter mixture into bite-size balls. Roll each ball in the rolled oats on all sides, and then set the balls some distance apart on a large plate. Cover loosely with plastic wrap, and refrigerate for 30 minutes.

5   Store in an airtight sealed container until ready to consume, up to one week.

Rice Pudding

I assumed a mercenary would be paid in gold. But according to the second-in-command of the Bull's Chargers, this is not always the case! One time, he, the Iron Bull, and five other Chargers defended a village from fifty bandits, an awe-inspiring feat by anyone's measure. I certainly listened in slack-jawed amazement as Krem recounted the tale. How incredible they must have been! If only I could've seen it for myself. Ahem. In any case, once the bandits were defeated and it came time for the Chargers to collect on the payment they were owed, instead of receiving a sack of gold, they got several bags of rice. When I asked what they did with all this rice, Krem only shrugged and said, "When life gives you rice, make rice pudding." I don't believe truer words were ever spoken!

Yield	Cook time	Difficulty
2 SERVINGS	40 MINUTES	AVERAGE

Ingredients

1¾ cups whole milk

Pinch of salt

2 tablespoons sugar

1 tablespoon vanilla extract

1 vanilla bean, with the core scraped out and retained

3.5 ounces short-grain rice

Squeeze of lemon juice

Cinnamon, for sprinkling

1   Combine the milk, salt, sugar, vanilla extract, vanilla bean, and scraped-out core of the vanilla bean in a medium pot. Bring to a boil over medium heat, stirring frequently.

2   Add the rice and carefully stir to combine. Reduce the heat to low and simmer, stirring constantly, until the rice is nice and soft and the mixture is creamy and smooth (about 30 minutes).

3   Remove from heat, stir in the lemon juice, and remove the vanilla bean.

4   Divide the rice pudding evenly between two small preheated bowls and sprinkle cinnamon on top.

Goat Custard

You'll find custards all across Thedas in a dizzying number of variations. I sourced this particular recipe from Rivain, where it has gained great popularity as a dessert. The custard is made from goat's milk and studded with roasted figs to add a touch of sweetness to the dish's overall richness. If you'd like to further enhance the dish's sweet flavors, milk from the Ayesleigh gulabi goat can be used, as it boasts a natural sweetness that makes it prized by custard connoisseurs everywhere.

Yield	Cook time	Difficulty
6 SERVINGS	75 MINUTES (INCLUDING STANDING AND SETTING)	AVERAGE

Ingredients

1⅔ cups goat milk

1⅔ cups heavy whipping cream

8.8 ounces fresh goat cheese

1 tablespoon honey, as thin as possible, plus more for drizzling (optional)

4 egg yolks

3 eggs

3 fresh figs

Equipment

Immersion blender

6 oven-safe dessert molds or ramekins (each with a capacity of about 7 ounces)

1 Combine the goat milk, cream, and goat cheese in a medium pot, and bring to a boil over medium heat, stirring frequently. Simmer for 1 minute. Remove from heat, and purée finely using an immersion blender. Add the honey and combine. Allow to stand for 20 minutes.

2 Beat the egg yolk and eggs with an electric mixer in a bowl (about 3 minutes). Add a little more than 3 tablespoons of the warm (not hot!) milk mixture to the eggs, and stir carefully to combine.

3 Preheat the oven to about 200°F. Arrange the dessert molds on a baking sheet.

4 Add the rest of the egg mixture to the milk mixture and stir a few times. Divide the cream evenly among the six dessert molds. Set the molds in the oven for about 35 to 40 minutes or until the pudding is firm, then remove them from the oven and allow the pudding to cool for several minutes.

5 Meanwhile, wash the figs, pat dry with paper towels, and slice with a sharp knife. Decorate the pudding with the fig slices immediately before serving. Drizzle with additional honey, to taste.

Baked Goods

Antivan Apple Grenade

It's no secret that I delight in creative presentations when it comes to food. Whether it's a crab cake designed to look like a crab or a dish featuring a fish peeking its head out of a pie, the extra touches are all certain to leave me clapping my hands with glee. Thankfully, this Antivan dessert nails it on both counts! Its name comes from the fact that it resembles the fire grenades reportedly used by the Antivan Crows assassins—not just in shape, but also in heat! I discovered that part for myself the hard way, when I bit into the piping-hot apple at the center of these sweet pastry bundles with a touch too much enthusiasm.

Contributor	Yield	Cook time	Difficulty
EMILY TAYLOR, SENIOR GAME DESIGNER	4 SERVINGS	50 MINUTES (INCLUDING BAKING)	AVERAGE

Ingredients

Dough

Scant 2 cups flour

1 teaspoon salt

12 tablespoons (1½ sticks) cold butter

Cold water, as needed

Filling

4 firm baking apples (Granny Smith or similar)

5.6 ounces fresh berries (raspberries or similar), quartered

1 tablespoon turbinado or raw sugar

4 tablespoons salted butter, divided

Ice cream or whipped cream

1   Sift the flour and salt into a bowl. Add the cold butter and use two small sharp knives to cut it into pea-size lumps. Add just enough cold water that you can work the ingredients (still using the knife) into a dough firm enough to roll out.

2   Use a rolling pin to roll out the dough as flat as possible. Then fold the sides in toward the middle, fold again, and refrigerate for a few minutes.

3   Meanwhile, prepare the filling. To do this, peel the apples with a small sharp knife, and carefully remove the core to hollow out each apple.

4   Preheat the oven to 425°F. Line a baking sheet with parchment paper.

5   Divide the chilled dough into four equal portions, then use a rolling pin to roll out each one into a rough circle on the counter. Set one apple in the center of each round of dough, with the opening facing up. Fill the apples three-quarters full with the berries, then top each with 1 tablespoon turbinado or raw sugar and 1 tablespoon butter.

6   Moisten the edges of the dough with a bit of water, then pull them together toward the top to encase the entire apple. Use your fingertips to press the seams together firmly over the apple to form a grenade-shape bundle. Cut away any excess dough with a knife. Cut a small hole in the top side of each bundle so the steam generated during baking can escape.

7   Set the apple grenades on the baking sheet and bake for about 30 minutes or until the apples are soft when pierced with a wooden skewer. Remove from the oven, and serve promptly with ice cream or whipped cream while the apples are still warm.

Found Cake

The Hero of Ferelden's mabari is very good at finding items. One time he even brought back a cake! As I understand it, the cake in question was of the chocolate cream variety, topped with white frosting and fresh strawberries. Of course, I had to try my hand at reproducing it, and I think the results are sure to delight. I did, however, make the decision to omit the few flecks of drool that apparently clung to the original. As much as we love our mabari in Ferelden, I don't think their spittle makes for a very appetizing ingredient. Not even Teyrn Loghain, who, I would argue, is far more tolerant of mabari drool than I, is liable to enjoy a cake that's become intimately acquainted with the inside of a mabari's mouth.

Yield	Cook time	Difficulty
1 CAKE (ABOUT 8 SERVINGS)	ABOUT 75 MINUTES (INCLUDING BAKING AND COOLING)	AVERAGE

Ingredients

Cake

9 tablespoons (1 stick plus 1 tablespoon) soft butter, plus more for the pan

⅓ cup sugar

3 eggs

1 teaspoon vanilla extract

1⅔ cups flour

2 teaspoons single-acting baking powder

2⅓ cups cocoa powder

¾ cup plus 2 tablespoons heavy whipping cream

Cream Cheese Frosting

14 ounces cream cheese, at room temperature

2 sticks plus 2 tablespoons butter, softened

1⅓ cups powdered sugar

1½ fresh strawberries, halved, for garnishing

Equipment

Springform pan (about 10 inches in diameter)

1   Preheat the oven to 350°F. Grease the springform pan.

To make the cake layers:

2   In a medium bowl, beat the butter and sugar with an electric mixer on medium speed until the mixture lightens in color (about 2 to 3 minutes). Add the eggs and vanilla extract, then continue beating for 1 minute.

3   Sift the flour, baking powder, and cocoa powder into the bowl. Add the cream and stir to combine.

4   Fill the prepared pan with batter. Smooth the top, and bake on the middle rack for about 35 to 40 minutes. Remove from the oven, and allow to cool for 10 minutes. Then carefully remove from the pan, and allow to cool completely.

To make the cream cheese frosting:

5   Transfer the cream cheese, butter, and powdered sugar to a bowl, and beat with a stand mixer or an electric mixer with the whisk attachment until creamy. Cover with plastic wrap and refrigerate until used.

To assemble:

6   Use a bread knife to carefully cut the fully cooled cake in half horizontally. Spread the bottom layer evenly with half of the cream cheese frosting. Set the top layer in place, and spread with the remaining frosting. Decorate with three strawberry halves (see picture), cover loosely with plastic wrap, and refrigerate until ready to serve.

Varric's Favorite Cinnamon Rolls

When you hear the tales of Thedas's heroes, what you don't always hear are the silly names Varric Tethras called them. Some of them more fitting—Blondie, Curly, Ruffles, Broody—and others a little more . . . ironic. Tiny? Chuckles? I can easily imagine his amusement at the exasperation of those around him, but that's Varric for you.

He can disarm anyone with his humor and charm (or quite literally, through his network of contacts).

I'll tell you a secret, though—I think he has a soft spot for the soft heroes. "Daisy" for Merrill, "Sunshine" for Bethany, "Kid" for Cole. I've even heard rumors that there was a kind, appeasing hero he called "Waffles." And "Waffles" is just one short step away from him calling someone a "Cinnamon Roll," which I've heard is one of his favorite sweets. (Some of these heroes would decidedly deserve that nickname, too.) I whipped up a batch of cinnamon rolls while thinking on it, and I believe they're the perfect treat to have while listening to him spin you a tale. Warm, sweet, comforting—the kind of treat not for listening to Hard in Hightown, but for hours spent reminiscing.

Yield	Cook time	Difficulty
8 TO 10 SERVINGS	2 HOURS 10 MINUTES (INCLUDING RISING AND BAKING)	AVERAGE

Ingredients

Dough
3½ tablespoons plus 5 tablespoons butter, divided

¾ cup plus 2 tablespoons milk

3¾ cups flour, plus more for the counter

½ teaspoon salt

1 teaspoon sugar

1 egg

3 tablespoons fresh yeast

Filling
3½ tablespoons soft butter, plus more for the pan

⅔ cup sugar

2 teaspoons ground cinnamon

Glaze
1 cup powdered sugar

3 tablespoons milk

Equipment
Casserole dish (about 8 by 12 inches)

To make the dough:

1 Heat 3½ tablespoons of butter and the milk in the microwave for about 10 to 15 seconds or until the butter has melted completely.

2 Transfer the flour, salt, sugar, and egg to a bowl. Make a hollow in the flour, and crumble the yeast in with your fingers. Pour the warm butter-and-milk mixture over it and knead all the ingredients together by hand until a smooth dough forms (about 5 to 6 minutes), starting near the hollow and working outward. If the dough is too sticky, gradually add more flour until the dough is pliable and smooth. Cover the bowl with a clean dish towel and allow the dough to stand in a warm place for 1 hour.

To make the filling:

3 Use a rolling pin to roll out the dough into a rectangle on a lightly floured surface, then brush the dough with butter. Combine the sugar and cinnamon in a small bowl and sprinkle evenly over the dough. Then roll up the dough from the long side, making sure not to squeeze too tightly, but also not to leave it too loose. Use a large, sharp knife to cut the roll of dough into slices about an inch thick.

4 Grease the casserole dish. Arrange the slices of dough, cut side down, seamlessly right next to each other in the pan. Cover the casserole dish with a clean dish towel and allow the dough to rise for another 30 minutes. Shortly before the end of the rising time, preheat the oven to 350°F.

5 Set the pan in the oven, and bake for about 15 to 20 minutes until the rolls are golden brown. Meanwhile, prepare the glaze.

To make the glaze:

6 Use a fork to whisk together the powdered sugar and milk in a small bowl.

To assemble:

7 Pour the glaze evenly over the top of the cinnamon rolls. Allow the glaze to dry before serving.

Croissants

The Orlesians certainly know how to make a good pastry! It's no wonder Lady Vivienne starts off her day with one of these, the most well-known of all Orlesian pastries and, in my humble opinion, the most delicious. But, by Andraste, these little crescents are a lot of work to make! In order to achieve that wonderfully flaky texture croissants are known for, the dough is layered with butter and then rolled and folded several times over before being rolled out into a thin sheet. It's times like these when I wish I had a strong companion like the Iron Bull or Commander Cullen to take over the duties with the rolling pin. Anything to spare my arms the indignity of being reduced to limp noodles!

Yield	Cook time	Difficulty
10 CROISSANTS	40 MINUTES (INCLUDING BAKING)	AVERAGE

Ingredients

18 ounces frozen puff pastry sheets (about 2 big sheets)

7 ounces marzipan

Flour for the counter

1 egg

1¼ cups semisweet chocolate

5 ounces almond crocant (caramelized nut crunch topping, store-bought) or other crocant, to taste

1 Thaw the puff pastry according to the instructions on the package.

2 Preheat the oven to 375°F. Line a baking sheet with parchment paper.

3 Knead the marzipan with your hands until it is pliable and shape into 10 equal balls.

4 Use a rolling pin to roll out the dough into a rectangle about 8 by 24 inches in size on a lightly floured surface. Cut the dough into 5 smaller rectangles, each about 4¾ inches wide. Cut each rectangle again diagonally so you have 10 right triangles.

5 Place a marzipan ball on the longer edge of each triangle, then roll up from the broad end toward the tip to make a croissant. Set the rolled croissants "tip" down on the prepared baking sheet, being sure to leave some space between them.

6 Beat the egg in a small bowl, and brush over the tops and sides of the croissants.

7 Bake on the middle rack for about 20 minutes. Allow the croissants to cool completely on the baking sheet.

8 Meanwhile, melt the chocolate either by using a double boiler or bain-marie or by heating it in 10-second intervals in the microwave.

9 Drizzle the chocolate over the croissants in a zigzag pattern and sprinkle to taste with almond crocant. Allow to dry briefly before serving.

Cherry Cupcakes

These delightful little cakes are decadence in bite-size form, as pleasing to the eye as they are to the tongue. Although they were served alongside other sweets, carried from one private box to the next by a servant on stilts at the Tevinter theater, I was so enchanted by the pink color that I barely noticed what else was on offer. It was only after I'd had a cupcake (or four) that I heard these tiny cakes were once used as a vehicle for deadly poisons! Thankfully, my cupcakes were poison-free, and so is the recipe I now pass on to you.

Yield	Cook time	Difficulty
12 CUPCAKES	45 MINUTES (INCLUDING BAKING)	AVERAGE

Ingredients

Batter
1½ cups flour

1 teaspoon single-acting baking powder

Pinch of salt

7 tablespoons butter, at room temperature

¾ cup sugar

2 teaspoons vanilla extract

2 eggs

⅔ cup milk

Filling
5.3 ounces sour cherries (from a jar or can), drained

3 tablespoons cherry juice (from the cherries)

3 tablespoons sugar

2 level teaspoons cornstarch

Topping
1 cup plus 2 tablespoons heavy whipping cream

3 tablespoons cherry powder (ground freeze-dried cherries, for example)

Equipment
12 paper muffin cups

Pastry bag with star-shape tip

To make the batter:

1 Preheat the oven to 350°F.

2 Combine the flour, baking powder, and salt in a medium bowl.

3 In a separate bowl, beat the butter, sugar, and vanilla extract with an electric mixer until creamy (about 2 to 3 minutes). Gradually add the eggs, milk, and flour mixture, combining well after each addition.

4 Set the muffin cups on a baking sheet and fill evenly with the batter. Place the baking sheet in the preheated oven, and bake for about 18 to 20 minutes until the cupcakes are golden. Remove from the oven and allow to cool completely. Meanwhile, prepare the filling and topping.

To make the filling:

5 Combine the sour cherries, cherry juice, sugar, and cornstarch in a small pot, and bring to a boil over medium heat, stirring occasionally. Simmer for 1 to 2 minutes, then remove from heat and set aside to cool.

To make the topping:

6 Combine the cream and cherry powder in a mixing cup or bowl and beat with an electric mixer until stiff peaks form (about 3 to 4 minutes). Transfer to a pastry bag or a freezer bag with one corner cut off (about ½ inch). Refrigerate until ready to use.

To assemble:

7 Use a large, sharp knife to cut the tops off the cupcakes so each one has a "lid." Then carefully hollow out each one in the middle, making sure the sides remain intact. Fill with lukewarm cherry filling, place the "lid" back on top, and use the pastry bag to squeeze some of the topping onto each cupcake.

8 Cover loosely with plastic wrap and refrigerate until ready to serve.

Chocolate Cake

I didn't have to travel very far to get my hands on this recipe. In fact, I didn't need to travel at all! This cake is actually one of Mum's recipes. She baked it for the first time on my tenth name-day, and it made for such a sweet celebration that not another name-day passed without me begging for an encore. Thankfully, Mum was kind enough to indulge me, even though, more often than not, she already had her hands full with the Couslands' meals. And so whenever I think about her love for me, this cake inevitably sits front and center in my mind. It therefore seems only fitting to include here.

Yield	Cook time	Difficulty
1 CAKE (ABOUT 8 TO 10 SERVINGS)	1 HOUR 45 MINUTES (INCLUDING BAKING AND COOLING)	AVERAGE

Ingredients

Cake

9 tablespoons (1 stick plus 1 tablespoon) butter, softened, plus more for the pan

¾ cup sugar

1 teaspoon vanilla extract

2 eggs

¼ cup currant jelly

1 cup plus 2 tablespoons buttermilk

1¼ cups flour

⅔ cup plus 1 tablespoon cocoa powder

1 teaspoon single-acting baking powder

1 teaspoon baking soda

½ cup plus 2 tablespoons chocolate chips or semisweet baking chocolate, roughly chopped

Ganache

1⅓ cups cream

1¾ cups chocolate chips or semisweet baking chocolate, roughly chopped

5½ tablespoons butter

8.8 ounces cream cheese

Equipment

Springform pan (about 10 inches in diameter)

To make the cake layers:

1 Preheat the oven to 350°F. Line the pan with parchment paper and grease the sides.

2 Combine the butter, sugar, and vanilla in a bowl, then beat with an electric mixer until creamy. Add the eggs one at a time, beating to combine after each addition. Then add the jelly and slowly stream in the buttermilk. Sift the flour, cocoa powder, baking powder, and baking soda over the mixture and fold in. Carefully fold in the chocolate. Transfer the batter to the prepared cake pan. Smooth the top, and bake for about 40 to 45 minutes or until a toothpick inserted into the middle of the cake comes out clean. Then remove the cake from the oven, allow it to cool for 15 minutes, and carefully remove it from the pan. Allow the cake to cool completely before frosting. Meanwhile, prepare the ganache.

To make the ganache:

3 Transfer the cream to a medium pot and bring to a brief boil over medium heat. As soon as bubbles form, remove from heat immediately and set on a trivet on the counter. Add the chocolate and butter and whisk, stirring occasionally, until both have melted. Allow the mixture to cool, stirring occasionally, until it is smooth and spreadable.

4 Beat the ganache with an electric mixer for about 2 to 3 minutes, gradually adding the cream cheese by tablespoons. The ganache should be as thick as possible, while still being spreadable.

To assemble:

5 Use a large bread knife to slice the cake horizontally into three equal layers. Set one of the layers on a serving plate and spread with an even layer of ganache a little less than half an inch thick. Set the second layer on top and spread this layer with the same thickness of ganache. Then set the third layer on top. Frost the whole cake, leaving a lot of texture. Refrigerate until served.

> For the best flavor, take the cake out of the refrigerator 30 minutes before serving so it can come to room temperature.

Varric's Favorite Pastries

Leave a plate of pastries, fresh from the oven, to cool on a windowsill, and you might soon find a certain member of House Tethras lurking nearby. It's unsurprising, given that the man's first thought when it came to renaming the Bone Pit was apparently "the pie fields."

I can't blame him, of course. I, too, love a good pastry, whether it be biscuit, roll, or bun. And after an extensive consultation with the famed arbalist himself, I've put together this sample, which is sure to delight! But whether you choose to leave them within dwarf's reach . . . well, that is entirely up to you.

Yield	Cook time	Difficulty
ABOUT 32 CANTUCCINI	ABOUT 50 MINUTES (INCLUDING BAKING)	AVERAGE

Ingredients

9 tablespoons butter, softened
3⅓ cups flour
1½ teaspoons single-acting baking powder
2 tablespoons vanilla extract
1 cup sugar
3 eggs
7 ounces whole almonds
Powdered sugar, for sprinkling

1. Combine the butter, flour, baking powder, vanilla extract, sugar, and eggs in a medium bowl and knead by hand or with a stand mixer until a relatively crumbly dough forms. Then knead in the almonds.

2. Preheat the oven to 350°F. Line two baking sheets with parchment paper.

3. Divide the dough into four equal pieces and shape each one by hand into a roll about 2 inches wide. Press down gently to flatten each one slightly. Place two strips on each baking sheet and bake on the middle racks for 25 minutes.

4. Carefully transfer the strips of dough from the baking sheet to a cutting board. While still hot, use a bread knife to slice each one into eight equal-size pieces. With the cut side down, set the pieces back on the baking sheets, and bake for another 10 minutes or until the cantuccini are golden brown and nice and crisp.

5. Sprinkle with a bit of powdered sugar before serving.

6. These cookies will keep for at least 4 weeks in an airtight sealed container.

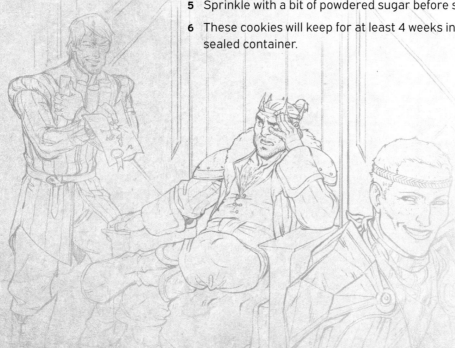

Sugar Cake

There's often joy in simplicity, as illustrated by this humble cake, which is topped with a sweet mixture of butter, sugar, and almonds. I purchased one off a surface dwarf merchant who assured me that it would be well received by any companion. According to him, even the Hero of Ferelden purchased a few for this very purpose. Of course, for me, traveling alone, this cake isn't as much a gift as it is the perfect pick-me-up after a long day of travel. But perhaps one day, I'll have a beloved companion to bake this cake for.

Yield	Cook time	Difficulty
1 SHEET CAKE (ABOUT 8 TO 10 SERVINGS)	ABOUT 2 HOURS 15 MINUTES (INCLUDING RISING AND BAKING)	AVERAGE

Ingredients

Cake

3 tablespoons fresh yeast, crumbled

1 teaspoon plus 7 tablespoons sugar, divided

1 cup plus 2 tablespoons lukewarm milk

4 tablespoons (½ stick) butter, melted

4 cups plus 2 tablespoons flour

Pinch of salt

Topping

1 pound (4 sticks) plus 3 tablespoons butter

5.3 ounces sliced almonds

¾ cup sugar

1 Combine the yeast, 1 teaspoon sugar, and milk in a bowl, stirring with a fork until the sugar and yeast have dissolved completely. Cover with a clean dish cloth and allow to stand in a warm place for 20 minutes.

2 In the bowl of a stand mixer fitted with a kneading hook attachment, knead together the butter, remaining sugar, salt, and yeast mixture until a smooth dough forms (about 5 to 6 minutes). Cover with a clean dish cloth and leave to rise in a warm place for 1 hour, or until the dough has doubled in size.

3 Line a baking sheet with parchment paper.

4 Knead the dough again for about 2 to 3 minutes, then roll it out evenly on the baking sheet with a rolling pin. Use your fingers to press indentations into the dough almost all the way through to the baking sheet.

5 To make the topping, sprinkle the butter over the indentations in flakes. Sprinkle evenly with the sliced almonds and sugar. Allow to stand for another 20 minutes.

6 Shortly before the end of the rising time, preheat the oven to 400°F.

7 Bake for about 15 to 20 minutes until golden brown.

Lamprey Cake

The lamprey is one of Thedas's more unique-looking creatures, with its long, slender body and toothed, suction-cup mouth. It's also one that's seldom found in the kitchen. Unless, of course, the kitchen belongs to Lord Norbert de la Haine, whose fondness for pickled lampreys was just as unfortunate as his desire to conquer the Free Marches.

Given that Lord de la Haine's tastes were rather singular, it's better, I think, to bring the lamprey to the dinner table in spirit only. Rest assured, you'll find none of its noxious flavors in this cake. I've limited myself to merely borrowing its shape.

Yield	Cook time	Difficulty
1 LAMPREY (ABOUT 6 TO 8 SERVINGS)	ABOUT 4 HOURS (INCLUDING BAKING AND COOLING)	DIFFICULT

Ingredients

Cake

5 eggs

1¼ cups sugar

1 teaspoon vanilla extract

3 cups flour

1 rounded tablespoon single-acting baking powder

½ cup plus 5 teaspoons neutral oil, such as canola or safflower

6 ounces orange soda

Butter, for greasing the pan

To make the cake:

1 Preheat the oven to 300°F.

2 Combine the eggs, sugar, and vanilla extract in a bowl and beat with an electric mixer for 2 minutes until creamy. Sift the flour and baking powder over the mixture and combine. Stir in the oil and soda.

3 Grease the springform pan, fill it with batter, and smooth the top. Bake on the center rack for about 50 to 60 minutes until golden or until a toothpick inserted into the middle comes out clean. Remove from the oven and leave in the pan to cool completely. Carefully remove the cake from the pan when you're ready to decorate it.

4 When the cake has cooled, cut two circles about 4 inches across out of the middle to make the "head." Then use a bread knife to cut the cake in half once horizontally and then cut the two cakes in half vertically. Set the individual pieces of cake (with the top and bottom sides still stacked) on a baking sheet lined with parchment paper or a large serving plate so that they are reminiscent of a twisting snake (see picture). Use a sharp knife to continue shaping the cake: To do this, round the sides a bit at the top and cut the "tail" so that it narrows more toward the tip. Stack the two head pieces, and place them in the appropriate spot. Refrigerate the cake until you're ready to assemble it.

To make the filling:

5 Beat the cream, powdered sugar,, and vanilla extract in a mixing bowl with a mixer until stiff (about 3 to 4 minutes).

6 Stir the sour cream in a bowl and add the strawberries. Fold into the whipped cream.

Continued on page 148

Filling

¾ cup plus 2 tablespoons heavy whipping cream

¼ cup powdered sugar

2 teaspoons vanilla extract

7 ounces strawberry pie filling

¾ cup plus 2 tablespoons sour cream

Decoration

21 ounces marzipan

Powdered sugar, for rolling out the marzipan

2 tablespoons strawberry preserves

1.75 ounces pine nuts, for the teeth

2 decorative fondant or sugar eyes

Black food coloring (liquid)

Food coloring in various shades of green (liquid)

Equipment

Springform pan (about 11 inches in diameter)

Food-safe paintbrush

7 Remove the top halves of the cake from the bottom halves. Spread the strawberry cream mixture evenly on the lower halves, and then replace the top halves, making sure to keep the "head" higher than the rest of the "snake." You can build up the "head" as needed with cake scraps.

To decorate the cake:

8 Knead the marzipan by hand until soft.

9 Sprinkle a bit of powdered sugar over the counter, then use a rolling pin to roll out the marzipan to a thickness of just less than ½ inch. Carefully lift the marzipan sheet with both hands and spread it over the entire cake. Gently press the marzipan into place on the cake, then cut away excess marzipan with a pair of scissors or kitchen shears.

10 Knead the excess marzipan, and shape it into a "fin." Set the fin on the inside of the cake and press on gently.

11 Carefully press a hollow into the top of the "head" at the center, and fill it with jam. Insert the pine nuts in a circular shape so they look like two rows of teeth. Place the decorative eyes at the sides. Use a toothpick to poke holes for the gills into the marzipan (see picture).

12 Brush black and green food coloring over the cake. Refrigerate for another 2 to 3 hours before consuming.

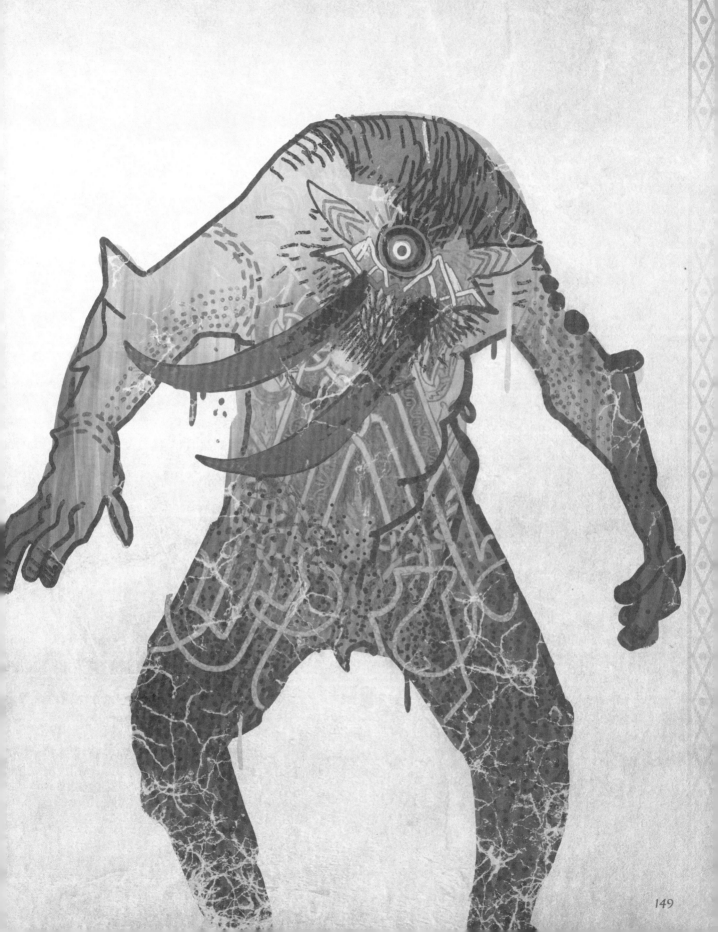

Tevinter Pumpkin Bread

Granted, I didn't need much tempting to visit Tevinter. After all, how else was I going to sample Dorian Pavus's favorites? But if I did require some convincing, these wonderful treats would certainly do the trick! Best of all, because the ingredients are so limited, I can share this recipe with more people than ever—provided, of course, I don't eat the whole pan by myself.

Yield	Cook time	Difficulty
1 LOAF	1 HOUR 35 MINUTES (INCLUDING RISING AND BAKING)	AVERAGE

Ingredients

10.5 ounces canned pumpkin

6 ounces pumpkin seeds (pepitas) and other seeds (such as chia and/or sunflower seeds), plus more, for sprinkling

5¾ cups plus 4 teaspoons flour, plus a bit more for the counter and the pan

3 tablespoons fresh yeast

1 teaspoon sugar

3 teaspoons salt

2¼ cups warm water

Also required:

Loaf pan (approximately 11 by 4 inches)

1 Place the pumpkin, mixed seeds, and flour in a large bowl. Crumble the yeast into the bowl with your fingers, add in the sugar and salt, and pour in the warm water. Using a stand mixer or an electric mixer with the kneading hook attachment, knead for about 5 to 8 minutes on medium speed until no visible flour remains.

2 Cover the dough with a clean dish cloth and allow to stand in a warm place for about 30 minutes, or until it has significantly increased in bulk.

3 Transfer the dough to a lightly floured surface and knead by hand for about 5 to 7 minutes. (This dough is relatively squishy; if it is too sticky, simply work in a bit more flour.)

4 Flour the loaf pan. Set the dough inside. Pull lengthwise if needed to fill the pan, then cover and allow to rise for another 10 minutes.

5 Meanwhile, preheat the oven to 400°F.

6 Sprinkle the dough with pumpkin seeds to taste and bake it on the center rack for about 40 to 45 minutes, cutting lengthwise with a small, sharp knife (about 1 inch deep) after about 10 to 15 minutes so the bread does not "break open." After the end of the baking time, remove from the oven and allow to cool completely, covered with a clean dish cloth, before removing from the pan.

7 Pairs wonderfully with Dwarven Plum Jam (see page 119).

Drinks & Potions

Lichen Ale

Deep underground, food is easily defined. So long as it's edible and capable of being scavenged, it'll eventually find its way into someone's stomach. That being said, the surface dweller's understanding of the word edible may not exactly align with that of an Orzammar dwarf. The best illustration of this is lichen ale, the drink of choice among the dwarves in Dust Town. Put simply, it is toxic, and I do mean that in the literal sense. In sufficient quantities, it can even overpower the heartiest of dwarven constitutions. As a result, the rest of us must approach this drink with caution. Although most can tolerate a few sips without issue, I think we'd all much rather enjoy a full glass of any beverage—particularly when we've made it ourselves. I, therefore, took it upon myself to devise my own rendition of lichen ale, using the dwarven recipe as a base. Now we can all enjoy the look and (most) of the flavors of the original without fear of poisoning ourselves in the process!

Yield	Cook time	Difficulty
1 DRINK	5 MINUTES	EASY

Ingredients

Handful of ice cubes

4 tablespoons vodka

5 tablespoons plus 1 teaspoon crème de cassis (blackcurrant liqueur)

2 tablespoons Kahlúa (coffee liqueur)

2 tablespoons ginger beer

Equipment

Cocktail shaker

1   Put the ice cubes in a cocktail shaker.

2   Add the vodka and both kinds of liqueur, close the shaker tightly, and shake vigorously for 10 to 15 seconds.

3   Strain into your desired glass without the ice, then pour in the ginger beer.

4   Serve immediately.

The Hissing Drake

During my visit to the Gilded Horn, I chanced upon a group of young men engaged in a contest of sorts. The goal? To drink as many Hissing Drakes as possible in quick succession, with the person who drank the most being crowned the victor. Evidently, they'd already had a few drinks before the idea occurred to them, as no sober individual would dare down more than a single glass of the stuff at a time due to its fiery effects on the stomach. In fact, when it comes to ill-advised drinking contests, I'd say this one is a close second to the game Admiral Isabela once played, with participants drinking based on the number of enemies they had. Suffice it to say, that one killed a man.

Thankfully, in this case, no one died. But I think the young men managed only two or three servings before they were forced to rush for the nearest balcony, where they were promptly divested of all their pride and bluster. I have no doubt that next time the urge to compete takes hold, they'll follow my advice and choose a soothing Fereldan ale instead.

Yield	Cook time	Difficulty
1 DRINK	5 MINUTES	AVERAGE

Ingredients

1 tablespoon plus 1 teaspoon lemon juice, plus more for garnishing

Sea salt, for garnishing

1 tablespoon plus 1 teaspoon vodka

4 tablespoons tomato juice

Squirt of Tabasco

Squirt of Worcestershire sauce

Pinch of pepper

Pinch of salt

1 celery rib, for garnishing

1 pickle, for garnishing

1 strip Spiced Jerky (page 31), for garnishing

1 Pour the lemon juice onto a shallow plate and sea salt onto another.

2 Turn over the glass and dip it in the juice so the rim is coated. Then press the moistened rim into the sea salt so the crystals stick to it.

3 Combine the vodka, tomato juice, Tabasco, Worcestershire sauce, pepper, and salt in a mixing glass or cup and stir thoroughly with a spoon.

4 Pour the mixture through a funnel into the prepared glass, leaving the salt rim intact.

5 Garnish with the celery, pickle, and Spiced Jerky and serve immediately.

Hot Chocolate

Varric isn't the only one who loves sweets. And, no, I'm not talking about myself; I'm talking about the Iron Bull! Hot chocolate is a particular favorite of his, to the point that it's practically a necessity. Although the cocoa powder he swears by is sometimes difficult to find, it's well worth the effort. Add hot milk and some Orlesian guimauves like the Iron Bull does, and you'll have a drink that's certain to please. Personally, I'm partial to topping it all off with a bit of whipped cream dusted with cinnamon, but there are many ways to dress up a cup of hot chocolate. So experiment!

Yield	Cook time	Difficulty
2 SERVINGS	10 MINUTES	AVERAGE

Ingredients

3 tablespoons plus 1 teaspoon heavy whipping cream

2¼ cups milk

2 tablespoons unsweetened cocoa powder

1 tablespoon vanilla extract

About ½ cup chocolate chips or semisweet baking chocolate, roughly chopped

Cinnamon, for sprinkling

1 Whip the cream in a mixing cup or bowl with an electric mixer on the medium setting until stiff peaks form (about 3 to 4 minutes). Set aside.

2 Combine the milk, cocoa powder, vanilla extract, and chopped chocolate or chocolate chips in a pot. Heat over medium heat, stirring constantly, until the chocolate is fully melted. Be sure to lower the heat as needed to keep the milk from boiling.

3 Remove the mixture from heat, allow it to cool for 2 minutes, and then stir thoroughly again and divide it evenly between two mugs or heatproof glasses. Top each with a generous dollop of whipped cream and serve sprinkled with a pinch of cinnamon.

Antivan Sip-Sip

I was warned that this particular drink packs a bit of a punch. More than "a bit," I'll say. Anyone capable of downing an entire glass of this in one go is made of sterner stuff than I! I could scarcely manage more than a small sip each time I brought this to my lips—and that was with the added help of a tall glass of water! Perhaps that's why it's called a sip-sip—because each sip of it must be chased with a sip of something else.

Yield	Cook time	Difficulty
1 DRINK	2 MINUTES	EASY

Ingredients

Handful of ice cubes

2 tablespoons coconut rum

2 tablespoons Jägermeister

2 tablespoons pineapple juice

Equipment

Cocktail shaker

1   Combine the ice cubes, rum, Jägermeister, and pineapple juice in a cocktail shaker. Close the shaker tightly and shake vigorously for 20 seconds.

2   Strain into a glass without ice.

3   Serve promptly.

Dragon Piss

I really do hope the name is figurative. It probably is—or, at least, that's what I'll tell myself now that I've sampled this less-than-enticingly-named drink. Perhaps the name Dragon Breath would suit it better? After all, it certainly burns like a dragon's breath—both in the glass and on the way down!

Yield	Cook time	Difficulty
1 DRINK	2 MINUTES	EASY

Ingredients

2 tablespoons Himbeergeist raspberry brandy (at least 80 proof, higher if you want to set the drink on fire)

4 teaspoons blue curaçao liqueur

Shot of sparkling wine

Equipment

Shot glass (large enough to hold at least 2.5 fluid ounces)

Lighter (optional)

1 Combine the raspberry brandy and blue curaçao in a shot class, and stir.

2 Carefully ignite, if desired.

3 "Extinguish" with a shot of sparkling wine and enjoy immediately.

Rivaini Tea Blend

A cup of tea is often the perfect accompaniment for any sweet treat, although it can certainly be enjoyed on its own. Personally, I'd still prefer the added biscuit on the side. Not just because I like desserts—I do, of course—but because it's great fun deciding which to pair with all the various blends.

When it comes to tea blends, the most famous is probably the classic Rivaini tea blend, a mixture of peppermint, lemon verbena, oregano, and licorice root. It's a wonderfully soothing combination that's said to have healing properties. In fact, I believe Empress Celene Valmont I of Orlais takes it throughout the day to alleviate headaches. Given how messy Orlesian politics are wont to be, with chevalier cousins vying for the throne and eleven handmaids turned both spymaster and lover, I imagine there must be a pot of the stuff boiling at all times!

Yield	Cook time	Difficulty
4 TO 5 POTS OF TEA	15 MINUTES (PLUS 3 HOURS FOR DRYING)	EASY

Ingredients

2 sprigs peppermint

1 sprig lemon verbena

1 sprig fresh oregano
(flowers and leaves)

Handful of fresh mixed edible flowers (such as elderflower, mallow, and marigold)

1 tablespoon
grated licorice root

1 vanilla bean, finely chopped

About 3.5 ounces black tea

Honey

Equipment

Mortar and pestle

1   Preheat the oven to 140°F. Line a baking sheet with parchment paper.

2   Spread the peppermint, lemon verbena, oregano, and mixed flowers in a layer on the baking sheet, and dry in the oven for 3 hours. During drying time, insert the handle of a wooden spoon into the oven door so that it stays cracked open and any moisture can escape.

3   After drying, carefully pick off the dried leaves and petals and dispose of the rest.

4   Using a mortar and pestle, roughly grind the plucked herbs.

5   In a small bowl, combine the grated licorice and vanilla bean with the black tea. Add the ground herbs and stir well to combine.

6   To prepare the tea, place 4 to 5 teaspoons in a tea ball and suspend the ball inside a teapot. Pour hot (not boiling!) water over the mixture and steep for 4 to 6 minutes, depending on how strong you like your tea. Then remove the tea ball. Ideally, pour the tea through a fine strainer so no residue gets into the cups. Sweeten with honey to taste and enjoy immediately.

This tea blend will keep for several months
in a small metal canister.

The Golden Nug

From the name, I expected this drink to be gold, but it's actually pink! Evidently, inspiration was drawn from the living creature rather than the golden statue I passed in Haven (of which I've heard there is more than one). A base of white Seleney wine sweetened with a splash of West Hill Brandy dilutes the color of the pomegranate juice and mulled raspberries into a softer, pinkish hue. The goal is to imitate the color of a typical nug, after all, not a severely sunburnt one!

Yield	Cook time	Difficulty
1 DRINK	3 MINUTES	EASY

Ingredients

Handful of ice cubes

5 tablespoons grapefruit juice

2 tablespoons plus
2 teaspoons gin

5 fluid ounces tonic water,
well chilled

1 sprig rosemary, for garnishing

1. Add the ice cubes to your desired glass.

2. Combine the grapefruit juice and gin in a mixing cup or other container. Pour over the ice, and then add the tonic water.

3. Garnish with a sprig of rosemary.

4. Enjoy immediately.

The Emerald Valley

The sisters of the Chantry truly make some marvelous creations—namely, the spirit used in this drink. Distilled from over seventy different herbs and flowers, it has a complex, varied flavor positively bursting with all the freshness of an emerald-green valley.

Yield	Cook time	Difficulty
1 DRINK	3 MINUTES	EASY

Ingredients

Handful of ice cubes

2 tablespoons bourbon

1 tablespoon plus 1 teaspoon herb liqueur

2 teaspoons simple syrup

1 tablespoon plus 1 teaspoon heavy whipping cream

1 egg yolk

Pinch of nutmeg, freshly grated

Equipment

Cocktail shaker

1 Put the ice cubes in the cocktail shaker.

2 Pour the whiskey, liqueur, syrup, and cream over the ice. Add the yolk to the shaker last. Close firmly and shake briefly and vigorously (about 10 seconds).

3 Strain the drink into your desired glass without ice, then sprinkle with a bit of freshly grated nutmeg and serve immediately.

> This recipe calls for a raw egg yolk, so make sure your egg is as fresh as possible.

Chasind Sack Mead

After having sampled some Chasind Wildwine, I wasn't surprised to learn that their mead is equally as strong. Some might even call it brutal. For me, the flavors are almost poetic. First, there's a near-overwhelming rush of honey, tinged with the sour-sweetness of apple blossoms, that fills the mouth with all the bright warmth of a summer's day. But as the initial sweetness fades, there comes an unexpected bitterness, reminiscent of the slow decay into fall, then winter. In essence, the turning of the seasons, all in a single cup—well, sack (although you can certainly fancy it up with a stunning decanter, as I've done here).

Yield	Cook time	Difficulty
ABOUT 100 FLUID OUNCES OF MEAD	2 HOURS (PLUS 9 WEEKS TO FERMENT)	DIFFICULT

Ingredients

25 fluid ounces apple juice (unfiltered)

2.5 grams pure culture brewer's yeast

85 fluid ounces water

53 ounces honey

1 gram yeast nutrient

25 grams St. John's wort

15 grams meadowsweet

10 grams verbena

1 to 2 milliliters kieselsol (from a pharmacy or brewer's supply store)

Equipment

Fermenter (with a capacity of about 5 liters) with a fermentation lock and rubber stopper

Thermometer

Glass bottles (for filling)

1 Sterilize the fermenter and all other utensils by thoroughly rinsing them with food-grade disinfectant and hot water. Then carefully rinse again with clean warm water.

2 Pour 1 cup plus 2 tablespoons of apple juice into a sterile glass, and carefully stir in the yeast. Cover the glass with a clean dish towel, and allow it to stand in a warm place for 90 minutes.

3 Meanwhile, bring the water to a boil in a large pot over high heat. Then remove the pot from the heat and allow the water to cool to below 77°F. Transfer the water to a large vessel together with the honey, the remaining apple juice, and the yeast nutrient; stir carefully to combine, and then fold in the yeast culture.

4 Funnel the mixture into the sterile fermenter. Add the St. John's wort, meadowsweet, and verbena. Tightly seal the fermenter with the rubber stopper, and leave it in a warm place to ferment for 4 weeks, swirling at least once daily during that time.

5 Allow the liquid to ferment for another 4 weeks, but this time without swirling. You can tell that fermentation is complete when you no longer see any bubbles rising in the fermentation lock. Now (and only now) is the time to open the fermenter and add the kieselsol, which causes the yeast to sink to the bottom. Then ferment for another week. To bottle, pass the mead through a fine sieve into the sterilized bottles. The mead will keep for about 3 months in airtight, sealed containers.

> Before fermenting, add a few blueberries, strawberries, or other fruits to produce nice colors and wonderful flavor variations.

Conversion Charts

Volume

U.S.	METRIC
⅕ teaspoon	1 ml
1 teaspoon	5 ml
1 tablespoon	15 ml
1 fluid ounce	30 ml
⅕ cup	50 ml
¼ cup	60 ml
⅓ cup	80 ml
½ cup	120 ml
⅔ cup	160 ml
¾ cup	180 ml
1 cup	240 ml
1 pint (2 cups)	480 ml
1 quart (4 cups)	1 l

Temperature

FAHRENHEIT	CELSIUS
200°	93.3°
212°	100°
250°	120°
275°	135°
300°	150°
325°	165°
350°	177°
400°	205°
425°	220°
450°	233°
475°	245°
500°	260°

Weight

U.S.	METRIC
0.5 ounce	14 grams
1 ounce	28 grams
¼ pound	113 grams
⅓ pound	151 grams
½ pound	227 grams
1 pound	454 grams

About the Authors and Photographer

Tom Grimm

Tom Grimm, born in 1972, apprenticed as a bookseller and has been working ever since as an author, translator, screenwriter, journalist, editor, and producer for a number of international publishers. Alongside his enthusiasm for literature, movies, and video games, he especially enjoys amusement parks, travel, listening to Rammstein, good food, bad jokes, and firing up the grill year-round. He is a passionate amateur cook, although not much of a baker. Even so, he has managed to win the Gourmand World Cookbook Award and other distinctions for his work. Tom lives with his family, a literal pride of cats, and several life-size images of Batman, Kung Fu Panda, Rayman, and Thrall the Orc. He lives and works in a small town in the west of Germany that is really and truly nothing to write home about. (Not kidding. Really.)

Dimitrie Harder

Dimitrie "Dimi" Harder was born in what is now the Central Asian country of Kyrgyzstan in 1977, the second child of a Russian mother and a German father. His home country is known for not only its magnificent mountain vistas and spectacular natural settings but also its cultural traditions of myths and sagas. Dimi moved to Germany with his family in 1990. It was here, in his newfound home, that he discovered his passion for photography, eventually turning what had been a hobby into a full-time job after stints as a melon picker, movie projectionist, pizza baker, and construction worker, among other jobs. With great patience and attention to detail, Dimi immerses himself in the mood and atmosphere befitting the worlds where he works with his images. He loves bicycling, running, hiking, and his motorcycle, detests food waste, and is the only person on earth ever to have officially referred to his "partner in crime," Tom Grimm, as a bully. (Which he definitely isn't— it's just that Tom can have a pretty big mouth at times!)

Jessie Hassett

Jessie Hassett is a recovering lawyer living in Toronto with her wife and two cats. She writes SFF with an emphasis on queer joy, telling stories full of magic, adventure, and, of course, kissing.

Published by Titan Books, London, in 2023.

TITAN
BOOKS

A division of Titan Publishing Group Ltd
144 Southwark Street
London SE1 0UP
www.titanbooks.com

 Find us on Facebook: www.facebook.com/TitanBooks

Follow us on Twitter: @titanbooks

INSIGHT
EDITIONS

Published by arrangement with Insight Editions, San Rafael, California, in 2023. www.insighteditions.com

A CIP catalogue record for this title is available from the British Library.

ISBN: 9781803367088

Publisher: Raoul Goff
VP, Co-Publisher: Vanessa Lopez
VP, Creative: Chrissy Kwasnik
VP, Manufacturing: Alix Nicholaeff
VP, Group Managing Editor: Vicki Jaeger
Publishing Director: Mike Degler
Art Director: Catherine San Juan
Design Manager: Megan Sinead Bingham
Executive Editor: Jennifer Sims
Associate Editor: Sadie Lowry
Managing Editor: Maria Spano
Senior Production Editor: Katie Rokakis
Production Associate: Deena Hashem
Senior Production Manager,
Subsidiary Rights: Lina s Palma-Tenema

Production Manager: Tom Grimm
Conception & Recipes: Tom Grimm
Text: Jessie Hassett
Photography: Tom Grimm & Dimitrie Harder
Design by: Dennis Winkler

Special Thanks to the Bioware Team
Matt Rhodes – Art Director
Mary Kirby – Editing
Ryan Cormier – Editing
Devon Gardner – Consumer Products Licensing
Carys Richards – Fan Experience Producer
Mad Bee – Fan Experience Producer

 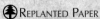

ROOTS of PEACE   REPLANTED PAPER

Insight Editions, in association with Roots of Peace, will plant two trees for each tree used in the manufacturing of this book. Roots of Peace is an internationally renowned humanitarian organization dedicated to eradicating land mines worldwide and converting war-torn lands into productive farms and wildlife habitats. Roots of Peace will plant two million fruit and nut trees in Afghanistan and provide farmers there with the skills and support necessary for sustainable land use.

Manufactured in China by Insight Editions

10 9 8 7 6 5 4 3 2 1